LOVE STYLES

Re-Engineering Marriage
for the New Millennium

Bryan Brook, Ph.D.

ProSe Associates, Inc.
Highlands Ranch, Colorado

Library of Congress Catalog Card Number:
99-75273

Printed in the U.S.A.

10 9 8 7 6 5 4 3 2 1

ISBN:0-9637285-3-9

Cover design by Dorothy Kavka

Acknowledgments

I wish to thank Phyllis Mendelson for her insights and time invested in the early drafts of the manuscript. Special thanks also to Lorel Powers for a splendid job of typing the final version of the book. I wish to acknowledge my one and only son, Kerwin Brook, who provides me much joy as he evolves personally and professionally. Also profound thanks to my late mother, Deborah Brook, who was always there, and to my father, Frank Brook, also deceased. Of course, great appreciation is owed to the courageous love style couples who've allowed their stories to be told. Joe Mierzwa, my literary representative, has been a tour de force with his expertise, guidance and belief in the project. Finally, my greatest appreciation to Jim and Cindy Thistel, whose loving friendship continues to nourish my spirit and personal growth.

Contents

Introduction

Near the end of the previous decade as one looked back on the 1980s, I crafted a somewhat pointed article entitled, "Designer Marriages: One Roof Does Not a Marriage Make." Written in 1989, I expressed my frustration with society's rigid adherence to a rather unbending, sanitized picture of marriage. Our most revered institution was in serious trouble, partly due to its own structural obsolescence. Yet no one was suggesting how marriage could become more responsive to today's complexity of diverse needs. Of course, there were psychological theory and therapy books galore which only viewed the marital landscape through a one dimensional lens. No one was offering a paradigm shift which reassembled the component parts so marriage might more realistically serve today's couples in their hour of greatest need.

The article garnered some media attention which led to the publication of "Design Your Love Life" and several national telecasts, including C.N.N. However, for the most part it died on the vine, just as so many marriages have, including my parents' and my own. How many toxic marriages and disrupted lives must there be before we wake up and smell the coffee? One roof...indeed one floor plan alone does not every marriage make. To help turn the tide:

Love Styles offers foresighted as well as distressed couples alike, validation to consider more customized options which can preserve their dreams before they turn into nightmares.

Love Styles seeks to expand our understanding of love life experiences with an entire spectrum of new concepts such as the mid-marriage emotional divorce or MED effect, the double downer or DUD effect, zombie marriages, modular marriage, modular monogamy, social architecture, time share marriages, condo couples, duplex marriages, etc.

Love Styles supports options which, hopefully, strengthen marriages and loving commitments so they can endure and beat the odds. While these imaginative models call for more flexible relationships, their foundation will always stand firmly planted in the top soil of traditional family values.

Love Styles also loudly applauds all spouses for whom more traditional marriage, perhaps reminiscent of the 1950's, is still the working model. However, today's embattled families and ominous divorce rates indicate that some traditionally tailored marriages may benefit from timely revision. For these distressed couples, more practical or inventive relationships could prove crucial at transitional phases in their lives.

Love Styles spotlights courageous couples who remain faithful to fundamental values and vows within uniquely remodeled relationships. These 21st Century marriage makeovers are illustrated by such creative couples today. In addition, permission and guidance is offered for those sufficiently interested to explore creative togetherness.

Love Styles also proposes sweeping social reform which virtually eliminates the courthouse divorce culture from America's matrimonial scene. The Annual Renewable Marital Agreement proposes all spouses renew their marriage license every year or simply "discontinue." This revolutionary aspect of ARMA formalizes what so many married couples take for granted on every anniversary.

ARMA affords them an annual marital check-up to consciously maintain, redesign or discontinue their shared lives.

Through expanded education, *Love Styles* seeks to elevate marriage back to the level of stability and reverence it once had and so richly deserves. Updating the institution, but never its values, hopefully ensures today's spouses and tomorrow's newlyweds will forever rejoice till death, not divorce, do them part. Couples can then experience creative togetherness for all eternity without any further need of annual renewal.

1 Marriage: A Crucial Crossroads

The courageous couples willing to live "outside the lines" to make their marriages work are the real love style pacesetters. They open our minds to creative alternatives many new millennium marriages may need in order to survive. Nourishing old world values while re-engineering new world models allows marriage as an institution to finally breathe, to spread its wings, even fly. Any institution must be considered a living symbol which requires constant vigilance. This is critical for any great society when one of its cornerstones begins to crack and crumble.

All right, already, enough doomsday philosophizing. Let's revisit the historical backdrop which sets the stage for the Love Style Revolution which awaits us at the gateway of the 21st Century. I conceived and wrote the following article "Designer Marriages" about a decade ago.

DESIGNER MARRIAGES:
ONE ROOF DOES NOT A MARRIAGE MAKE

Whether someone is married, single, divorced or widowed, today's sociological landscape resembles more a mine field than a lily field. Everyday the media bombard us with stories about updated social casualties. The U. S. Census Bureau declares nearly one-third of women ages 35 to 39 are already divorced. We are informed that 60% of women who marry in their 30's will probably divorce during their lifetime. In addition, for women who marry in their 20's, the projected rate of divorce is 50%.

Matrimonial panic for many women occurred when Yale sociologists Patricia Crane and Neil Bennett, along with Harvard economist David Bloom, polled 1,500 households from a 1980 U. S. Census Bureau sample of 70,000 homes. Their Yale-Harvard study was misinterpreted in the press. Women age 30 were sentenced to lifetime odds of just 30% for marriage, while those at 40 had less than a 3% chance at matrimonial bliss. Newsweek Magazine placed women over 40 in their social obituary when they published the odds for them finding Prince Charming at less than going through a terrorist attack. Thanks to 27-year old Susan Faludi's investigative reporting for the San Jose Mercury News, such journalistic terror was soon corrected. Women actually had a 66% statistical chance at marriage by age 30, and a 23% shot when life begins at 40.

Just when you thought it was safe to get back in the water, we hear of other disturbing national trends. Both marriage and divorce continue to be popular in this country with approximately 2.5 million marriages and 1.25 million divorces recorded annually. Although the huge post-World War II baby boom generation still maintains its high annual level of marriages, single women generally have dramatically altered the picture. In fact, the marriage rate for single women ages 15 to 44 was 99.3 weddings per 1,000 single females in 1983, the first time this measure has ever dipped below 100. The National Center for Health Statistics reports the highest marriage year for single women was 166.4 weddings per 1,000 single females in 1950.

The Census Bureau also notes nearly 15% of women born in the 1950's have not married at all. In 1986, 56% of American women ages 20 to 24 years remained unmarried. In 1984, the median age for marriage climbed to 23 years for women and 25.4 years for men. No doubt concerns about career, but also caution over marriage and economics are at play here. To set the record straight, there are reportedly 47.6 million single women and men over age 25 in the United States who have not married, including 25.9 million males. Women, however, exceed men in all other singles' categories, including separated, divorced and widowed. The discrepancy is most critical between the ages of 30 and 54, where there are 1.5 million more single women.

For the past several decades, since the advent of contraceptives and the sexual revolution, more men and women have chosen not to marry for sex. In 1987, less than 15% of American women waited for marriage to begin sexual activity, according to the National Center for Health Statistics. Another study at John Hopkins University shows the average age for first engaging in sex is just 16.2 years for women and 15.7 for men.

In addition, medical technology now permits increasing numbers of women to give birth without benefit of either intercourse or marriage. Advances in artificial insemination, in vitro fertilization, etc., allow women who are disinterested or afraid of marriage to utilize an anonymous donor's sperm in order to become a mother. Other women still have sex the old-fashioned way but may or may not tell their partner about the agenda to get pregnant.

According to sociologist Pepper Schwartz, such trends continue to steadily undermine the institution of marriage. Many women today are also deciding to remain single longer, date younger men or have affairs with married men, if they choose to relate with men at all. Thus, traditional practices of finding a man and getting married for child bearing and rearing are no longer a priority for some women. Marriage is no longer forever, or "til death do us part." The National Center for Health Statistics reports that the average life span of American marriages is seven years. In the 1980's, 45% of

13

all marriages in the U.S. are remarriages. Approximately 80% of divorced men and 75% of divorced women get remarried. Tragically, the divorce rate for remarriages is even higher than the 50% reported level for first-time marriages. Still, many Americans commit and recommit to marriage, but frequently with a more cynical, defensive attitude for each new partner. In spite of statistics, 90% of previously unmarried young Americans when surveyed, still expect to blissfully, marry "til death do us part." Thus, many of us wear blinders while "married" to the traditional, conjugal stereotype of marriage. To say that contemporary men and women are a little suspicious of each other's motives is understatement on the grandest scale. Palimony lawyers, paternity suits, prenuptial/postnuptial/non-marriage agreements only convey the very tip of the interpersonal iceberg when couples negotiate matrimony. Common law and trial marriages are yet another variation on the ambivalent theme of "let's be committed without being committed." That's like saying let's get a little married and a little pregnant.

It is estimated in 1987 that more than two million unmarried heterosexual couples live together in the U.S. This represents a fourfold increase since 1970. One might expect the results would be more successful than marriage. However, most of the perils of traditional marriage appear to equally occur with common space or common law marriages. In addition, trial marriages in which couples live together before tying the knot show the same discouraging divorce rates as marriages without the dress rehearsal.

Many adults by age 35 appear to have some distrust of society's marriage system and of each other's matrimonial motives. Perhaps one of your best lady friends or buddies got taken to the cleaners in divorce court. They either lost their homes, custody of the kids, pay child support or temporary maintenance. Or maybe your sister left her husband after three years when she literally uncovered his extra-marital affair. She got her divorce and now hopes to find a new husband to love and help support her and the baby. She's

30 years old, young and attractive, but she's shocked at just how unmarketable she is in today's marriage market place. We've all heard the stories or, perhaps, painfully lived them. Have television soap operas created the scenarios for real-life marriages, or has this country's marriage system produced the script for our make-believe media? Lines between the two have all but faded. Our religious institutions, justice system, advertising industry and government all proclaim the benefits and necessity of conjugal marriage as the cornerstone of society. Unfortunately, real life conditions which actually motivate many marriages include making parents happy, premarital pregnancy, economic insecurities, relationship-ending ultimatums, inflated egos, deflated egos, leaving home and fulfilling society's script for our lives. These are never the best circumstances under which to love, cherish and "obey" anyone.

AIDS is the black plague revisited. Perhaps it is Nature saying we have expanded the biological bubble of our sexual revolution beyond its limits. Our immune system cannot cope. By 1991, the Center for Disease Control forecasts AIDS will strike 270,000 Americans, with 179,000 dying. Another 54,000 are projected to die of AIDS in 1991 alone, killing more people than automobile accidents. However, AIDS should not be used to panic or stampede people into marriage. The cultivation of safe sexual friendships may begin to make sense here. Safe sex friendships would include sex between AIDS antibody-free persons who wish to be friends and nothing more. However, loving relationships within the context of designer marriage would seem to offer a safer and more fulfilling prospect. Designer marriage provides an alternative path to meet one's need for freedom, safety and intimacy. Designer marriage describes a very traditional, loving relationship which is sexually exclusive and emotionally committed. It is also non-traditional since it is not legally binding and partners usually remain residentially separate. It is in effect an emotional, spiritual marriage.

Designer marriage is not sequential in its expectations where boy meets girl, they fall in love, get married, have kids and live happily ever after, or get divorced. These men and women feel more secure with a residentially separate, sexually exclusive commitment between lovers than perhaps many who are maritally homebound. Each partner continues to remain solely responsible for his or her own life.

Some may point out that designer marriage is nothing more than extended dating. On the contrary, designer marriage is marriage based on love, trust and commitment. It seeks to incorporate the best and eliminate the worst of court-bound marriage. Others may think designer marriage encourages sexual dishonesty behind each others' backs. Research estimates of extra-marital affairs range from 25% to 75% of married couples. Thus, mainstream marriage offers us little safeguard from infidelity or AIDS.

Why, then, do so many husbands and wives pursue sex outside their marriage vows? Most people apparently do not understand that mature love begins when passion plateaus. They find it exceedingly difficult to keep their sexual and loving feelings enriched after several years of marriage. Monogamy becomes monotony. Feeling trapped and seeking sexual variety frequently overcomes the sense of loyalty or religious values. Carol Botwin, author of "Is There Sex After Marriage?", claims it is normal for sexual frequency to decline to about 50% of its original level after several years of marriage. Americans readily change their jobs, houses and hometowns. We move on the average of once every five years. Perhaps, not coincidentally, the first few years of marriage tend to be the happiest we recall. Unfortunately, when passions subside, bills mount, daily hassles increase and kids appear, marriage, for many, becomes another disposable item. By living and loving in separate residences, designer marriage offers mutual sexual anticipation instead of using someone for sleeping pill sex at night. Lack of day-to-day familiarity reduces the breeding of sexual, let alone personal contempt. Romantic bonding replaces legal bondage while reducing erosive hassles over interpersonal control.

Sociobiologists argue that man's predatory sexual heritage was the key to perpetuating the human species. Once mating occurred, the female took care of the offspring. "Unbonding" was necessary to force the male to move on to other fertile females to plant another human seed. However, today's vasectomized males, divorced fathers, childless by choice or infertile men have little biological urge to expand the species, as is also true for millions of their female counterparts. Their primary goal now is to merely sustain a mutually caring loveship.

Designer marriage also offers better odds for avoiding personal ruts and sexual routines. Men and women are supported to develop and maintain separate friends and activities, while other ones are still shared. Partners have no hidden agendas to be taken care of economically. They do not strive to entrap, control or change each other. There is no desire to fulfill their daily "Okayness" ration through a spouse or to legitimize their affections to society. The mutual survival game of two immature identities using the sanctuary of marriage in which to hide is avoided. Respect for each other's individuality is more highly valued in designer marriages than seems apparent or even possible given the stressful logistics of contemporary dual career marriage.

Stop for a moment to ask yourself a few questions. How many traditionally married couples share what you consider to be a vital, loving life together? How many after two years? Five years? Ten years? How many have divorced, are divorcing, or should divorce? How many have emotionally divorced but still live together? If you share the experience of many people today, you get the sad point.

Are designer marriages anti-social? They certainly are anti-traditional, even radical-traditional. However, it cannot be anti-social to foster a more realistic way to have loving, stable relationships. It is, however, criminal to promote a milieu which produces spousal homicide, child abuse, sexual control and psychological warfare. In "Behind Closed Doors," author Murray Straus and his fellow researchers surveyed a random sample of 2,143 marriages in their study subtitled, *Violence in The American Family*. They found that one out of eight married couples experienced at least one beating incident in the course of their marriage which required some form of medical attention. For a majority of these couples, the violence started only after they were married. In addition, another study of domestic violence discovered that a large number of attacks by husbands seemed to occur when the wife was pregnant, also posing added danger to the yet unborn child.

Straus' research determined that about one out of 26 American wives are beaten by their husbands every year. This projects to a minimum of 1.8 million wife beatings per year. However, unexpectedly, each year one out of 22 women also violently attack their husbands which calculates to more than two million violent events. It appears unrealistic and inadvisable for many men and women to cope with the overwhelming frustrations of contemporary conjugal life. Designer marriage proposes an alternative to the traditional conjugal cycle of control, frustration and violence, at least where children are not presently involved.

However, there are certainly some couples who seem to thrive on marriage. They can live and love together and still maintain individual selfhood. They show minimal need to dominate one another. They know how to let up, out of respect and mature love. They are personally secure as people and do not look to someone else to make them whole. It is 1 + 1 = 2, *not* ½ + ½ = 1, which occurs all too frequently in contemporary marriage.

Designer marriages strive for 1 + 1 = 2 PLUS. This occurs when two whole persons create a bond that is greater than the sum of the partners. The need for intimacy is the need to know and be known. Psychologist Dan McAdams contends that our need for power and control fights our need for closeness. "In a relationship you have essentially two life stories and someone has to be open for overlap," he writes. For the fortunate few, conjugal marriage provides a harmonious blend of power and intimacy. For others, there develops more of a blender effect which mixes these needs into a conflictual brew with the bitter aftertaste of divorce.

Someone recently posed the challenge that the vast majority of American marriages refute the need for any sort of new marital model. Unfortunately, just staying married, or marriage longevity, has never been a reliable indicator of marital satisfaction. Even couples who've remained married for 50 years may do so for various dubious factors such as: (1) economics, (2) children, and (3) fear of the unknown. It is at best an assumption that those who've remained married do so out of growing, loving contentment. The test of time can sometimes be nothing more than a test of endurance. Designer marriage is not really a new concept, although it has not been previously labeled and defined. It is based on old-fashioned virtues of love, respect and trust. It relies heavily on sexual fidelity, emotional commitment, and shared spirituality.

Today, one out of every three children in the United States will watch their parents divorce. There are more than 11 million American children who currently live in the crossfire of divorce. One out of every four homes in 1986 was headed by a single mother. While it does sound quite radical, perhaps some designer marriages would stay residentially separate even if children were born. However, a formal marriage decree would then need to protect the children's rights. Both emotional marriage and parenthood may be better served for some couples with this strategy. Some husbands/fathers and wives/mothers may actually invest more of themselves in such roles than when they are environmentally obligated.

The essence of designer marriage is to rethink marriage in order to strengthen individual growth and interpersonal love. It invites men and women who have socially given up or withdrawn to return to a more realistic and accessible form of emotional commitment. It encourages women and men for whom parenting, for the most part, is no longer an issue to be less paranoid about future loving relationships even if they are financially and emotionally bankrupt from a prior divorce. Designer marriage totally rules out casual sex and supports new couples being AIDS tested. In doing so, men and women are empowered truly to be the architects of intimacy in their lives.

Since writing this article, another decade has passed, but not much has changed. Every year, well over a million U. S. couples who once proclaimed a lifetime of undying devotion still get divorced. American marriages in 1999 now average about 6.4 years, while remarriages typically end eight months sooner. During the past century, one out of every four persons who has ever married in this land has divorced. That's nearly 50 million well intentioned people who pulled the plug on their dreams. Yet we still want to believe true love lasts forever. Amazingly, about 80% remarry (5% to the exact same person), and then almost always go back to the same old marital mold.

Surely, a case can be made that Americans, as well as much of the world, suffer from some mysterious ailment of the heart. Symptoms include romanticized or predatory dating, sexual addictions, exploitive relationships, intimacy disabilities and marital malaise. Is it any wonder we see marital infidelity and divorce in epidemic proportions? **Our throw away society tries to recycle what was once a sacred bond.** This also includes countless long term committed relationships which are discarded everyday, for which statistics do not exist. However, marketing traditional marriage as an idealized fairytale has blossomed into an annual $35 billion industry. Rebuilding after the destructive force of divorce's funnel cloud hits home, also generates its own $50 billion cottage industry every year. That's some kind of cottage!

2 Adapting Marriage to the 21ˢᵗ Century

We can only hope people truly benefit from the vast array of self-help books, tapes, workshops, seminars and infomercials devoted to creating real love. Couples counseling, marital therapy, premarital counseling, sex therapy, family therapy and support groups attempt to deal with the issues. Churches and other spiritual resources are also frequently called upon to lend a helping hand. Even psychics are consulted about what to do. Sometimes troubled marriages are saved, but all too often it's too late. Too much pain has been endured. Too much damage has been done.

However, one remedy for the devious "love virus" remains vastly unexplored, if not mostly ignored, by both professionals and the public. **This missing link in the battle to preserve family values and lasting love includes the entire arsenal of social architectural options. What was once considered the aftermath of the problem may actually be part of the solution.** This, of course, calls for more realistic models of marriage, where a monogamous couple may choose to live with more autonomy under the same roof, or under different roofs entirely.

When we consider that nearly half of this country's 2.5 million marriages every year are remarriages, it seems imperative to study more flexible models for family and married life. What was expected from the institution of marriage in 1900, is now little more than a mirage compared to what marriage demands from us in the year 2000. Just as today's technology turns over every few years, living designs for families and couples also require revision when traditional ones no longer work. However, while it may be necessary to redesign the vehicle, passengers need not be summarily cast off along the way.

Hopefully, what will never change are those traditional values from the past which need to be embraced now more than ever. Today's moral compass still points toward mutual monogamy, respect, trust, responsibility and religious spiritual practice with mature loving devotion to family. However, old fashioned marital styles need updating to give loving couples and families a fighting chance in the new millennium. **We've reached a crucial crossroads between marital illusion and what it truly takes for loving commitment and marriage to succeed in a constantly changing hi-tech world.**

For example, let's meet one of those couples who've worked very hard on the quality of their family life. Joan and Stan are a dual career couple married six years, who live with four year old daughter, Patti. They've invested considerable time and expense trying to improve their communication skills via therapy and workshops. Unfortunately, serious conflict still persists as each frequently feels manipulated and controlled. Family tensions heighten as each side lobs one missile after another with no truce in sight. **Even though Joan and Stan remain married, they more accurately "live in a divorce."** While not counted in Census Bureau divorce statistics, they represent millions of embattled households. Tragically, spousal verbal abuse, battering, child abuse, homicide and suicide have become all too commonplace where distressed couples feel they have no other way out.

Should lovemates, socially programmed to live together as roommates, be doomed to feel like cellmates? What was envisioned as a palace of eternal bliss has for some become a chamber of marital horrors, not at all what the bridal industry would have us believe. While many loving couples live together traditionally and in relative harmony, others require more spacious ways to maintain their devotion. Otherwise, they feel paralyzed by their own fragmented world of marital stereotypes and realities. The 21st Century will require a truly evolving marital blueprint with far more than just one "cookie cutter" approach to committed love.

Fortunately, there are a growing number of courageous, if not unconventional couples who've discovered that passionate commitment is nourished when time, space and responsibility are tailored to what feels right for them. They are unafraid to change living logistics when experience over time dictates they do so. They have learned to survive, even thrive, with more functional love styles than most of us have dreamed of. In essence, their love lives are "custom fitted." As more pliable and resilient marriage makeovers prove successful for greater numbers of couples, family life in the future will also, hopefully, benefit.

Although we proclaim otherwise, many of us cling tightly to the notion our life mates and marriages will stay essentially the same "til death do us part." Those who harbor such notions tend to be fear and security driven. The real trick is to balance mutual dependency with an expanding need for autonomy and self-expression. Just how limited is the range of options a couple sees as available before breaking off their relationship and losing all they have invested? Perhaps it's really the relationship design which could use a tweak at times, not one's choice of mate. After all, we don't routinely change cars when one only needs a tuneup.

Social architecture's redesigns of how we share time, space and responsibility with loved ones, offer unique solutions for couples who feel burned out. Rearranged relationships correct shared space hassles, power struggles and life style conflicts which prove the undoing of so many.

Social architecture's sole purpose is to help foster a couple's desired level of intimate independency.

As a matter of fact, many of America's 65 million married couples in 1999 already have, in effect, marital redesigns which diverge from yesterday's norms. Separate beds, bedrooms, vacations, bank accounts and friends are just a few. These were once considered signs of a troubled or bohemian marriage, while today they've become the norm. Today's cutting edge couples who choose to negotiate more limited togetherness qualify as a **Time Share Marriage**. Examples include Neighborhood Spouses, Duplex Marriage, Sidekick Apartments, Weekend Marriage, Rotating Parenthood Apartment Marriage, Condo Couples, and emptynest-Winnebago marriages.

Marital redesigns should be considered only after other conventional approaches. A once married couple, now divorced, live together quite successfully. Another divorced couple, who have remarried each other, are doing just fine living apart. **Love styles help couples evolve, not dissolve, by going the extra mile.** They are not intended to escape responsibilities which play a key part in every committed relationship. They merely offer other ways of sharing time, space and connection, which can be beneficial to some disheartened couples. Otherwise, they remain stuck in couples' "limbo land" where they co-exist, uncommitted to either staying married or getting divorced.

Whether you are happier living on different floors of the same house, across the street or across town can be determined only by you and your beloved. One model, definitely, does not fit all when it comes to personal love styles. Now here's a glimpse at several love style choices being lived out by today's new millennium couples.

SEPARATE BEDROOMS

In the past, separate beds, let alone separate bedrooms, were viewed as a marital death blow, where sex and the marriage were over. However, Hank and Jill actually choose separate bedrooms to keep passion aglow. This redesign also addresses their disparity in sleep rhythms, as well as health concerns, when one or both is sick. Keep in mind both enjoy cuddling very much before going to sleep, whether they make love or not. Having their own bedrooms actually has enhanced their sense of connection and intimacy while offering nights of restful sleep.

WEEKEND MARRIAGE

Seeing each other only on weekends increases the risk some persons will emotionally distance and have affairs. However, for Jeff and Arlene, the weekend has become a special time for deepening their love. During the week, they pursue their own geographic career priorities. **Sexual tensions, instead of marital tensions, build until the weekend arrives.**

ROTATING PARENTHOOD APARTMENT MARRIAGE

Every two weeks Jackie and Ted take turns as primary parent, living at home with the kids, or alone in a "retreat" apartment. They remain "sexclusive" lovers, but now with the twist of courting once again. As re-energized parents, they bring their best back home to the children following their parenting vacations. Living apart, they are no more likely to engage in affairs, than living together ensures fidelity. In fact, living apart has actually strengthened their commitment, both as a married couple and family. The parent on vacation also returns home at times for family meals and activities. Jackie reminds us, "it's so much better to court each other, than take each other to court."

INTENTIONAL FAMILY MARRIAGE

This is the unique story of two married monogamous couples, the Heads and Hoags, who bring new meaning to the term love styles. They choose to live together as one family, under one roof, in a house they all have purchased. The Heads also have a six year old son who gets to have four loving parents. This redesign succeeds because they know how to compromise creatively. Laying aside the myth that more people only dilute a couple's connection, this Intentional Family Marriage generates abundant supportive resources, so everyone has more to offer their intimate partner.

Before we get ahead of ourselves, however, let's trace our steps in the sand to understand just how The Great American Marriage Fantasy came to settle on the shaky ground it stands on today.

3 Cohabiting:
Fantasy vs. Reality

Compare, for a moment, life in the 1950's with life today. Back then, wives and husbands lived relatively uncomplicated lives as homemaker and breadwinner. Prescribed roles were clear from the start. Marriage meant a son and daughter, a house in the suburbs with a red, white and blue picket fence, a dog named Rex and a shining new Ford. When the kids moved out, Susie found volunteer work or even returned to school. After 40 years with the company, Tom traded in his briefcase for a fishing pole. "The good life" was providing the kids more than their parents ever dreamed for themselves.

The doting mother and attentive wife of yesterday needs to be a superwoman today. She juggles a husband, two kids, four travel agency work days, daily fitness class and night study for her real estate license. Her penchant for crossword puzzles is now an occasional luxury, as is reading, writing letters, taking a bath and even having sex. Today's dedicated husband also carries a staggering lifeload: working, working out, commuting, parenting, investing and, of course, networking on the golf course and the Internet. Arriving home by 7 p.m. leaves little time for family, let alone romantic dinners or a movie. After looking over the mail and watching TV sports, he's nodded off for the evening. Despite all the time saving gadgets and conveniences, couples are sometimes lucky to share even a few minutes of rollover sex. Any vestiges of gourmet lovemaking departed somewhere between the first anniversary and the first born.

As we race headlong into the 21st Century, we need to fast forward our TV soap opera and romantic movie versions of cohabiting. As boys and girls we were seldom taught adaptive skills to help us live together. Cohabiting 101 is not listed on anyone's curriculum vitae. Growing up, we were simply groomed for our respective roles as woman and man of the house. Women living in the 1940's and 1950's learned to change the sheets once a week, clean the litter box once a week, and change the diapers more than once every hour. Granted there are a few women out there who know as much about fixing leaks, changing oil filters or calculating earned run averages as any man. Most, however, don't. There's also the occasional '90's man who lives to iron his shirts, decorate his apartment and make a great soufflé. He's also a rare commodity.

We frequently just don't understand each other's private worlds. No matter what generation we were born into, he'll still never know what it's like to have a period, menopause or cellulite. While, thank heaven, she'll never experience male impotence, performance anxiety or a beer belly. Specific idiosyncracies of every individual just add to the mix, so that mating becomes a mystical equation of serendipity and creative visualization.

THE URGE TO MERGE

We move in together and attempt to mesh but not enmesh our lives. Not a simple task when his furniture is vintage Salvation Army and yours is custom contemporary. His wardrobe is an eyesore and yours a sight for sore eyes. He would starve without a microwave and McDonald's. You? Well, so you're not Julia Child, but you can at least boil water, iron a shirt and sew on a lousy button! To be fair, the poor dear had no clue he'd be the guinea pig for your next book, *Tofu*

365 Ways. In the beginning, you had everything in common from music to movies, sun signs to star gazing. It couldn't have been a better match. He was the missing piece to your life's puzzle, the love connection you always believed would someday show up and make you whole.

Since cohabiting, however, all you see are the jagged edges. Where were the tattered tee shirts, psychedelic sweaters, Playboy magazines and striped orange socks before? And those lamps! What planet did they come from? Mars! Of course! His atrocious furniture has invaded your esthetically designed living space. As much as you wish you could throw his "stuff" out, it's now part of your life, like it or not. Just as your makeup, lotions, potions, curling iron, blow dryer, jewelry tree, cabinet of vitamins, foods he's not allowed to touch and foods he'd never want to touch are now part of his life.

You invited him to move into your apartment because it was twice the size and half the cost of his. Double the space or not, it can't possibly accommodate two sets of furniture, three kinds of dishes and four cats. Your closets are already maxed out and he hasn't even begun to unpack his crates of personal items and sports equipment. A match made in heaven? How about one from a much warmer climate, roughly 180 degrees in the opposite direction!

Putting two people together is like a chemistry experiment: sometimes the reactions blow up in your face. Not until we merge our lives, do we realize how volatile the formula can be.

Living together harmoniously is about as easy as getting a guy to part with his remote. The fact that your lover snores is neither good nor bad. It only becomes a problem when it starts to affect the quality of your sleep. Just because you like to read in bed with the light on while he tries to sleep is not negative behavior, unless it bothers him. When we describe behaviors as positive or negative, we screen them through our own highly subjective filter. All that really counts is the meaning we make of each other's actions. What you consider childish behavior may be viewed as playful, fun energy by someone else. It's important to understand your partner's need to express in their chosen way. It takes conscious effort not to judge, but instead reflect what a particular behavior brings up for you. This helps avoid the #1 Public Enemy of relationships...the Blame Game. **Remember, if you want to keep the love you have, it's more important to be together than right.**

There are certainly extraordinary spouses who can share full time togetherness in a mutually supportive manner. Such couples are on the marital endangered species list. They illustrate how it is possible to avoid major power struggles, and balance intimacy with autonomy at work, home, and play. Some even work with each other in the same profession as joyful collaborators. For them, marriage has become a celebration of co-creation, not competition. These marriages stand in stark contrast to those where spouses dread just being in each other's presence. In reality, there are very few couples capable of full time togetherness, where they can navigate smoothly around and through one another's boundaries.

To stay a loving couple, we must optimize what works in a relationship and minimize what doesn't. We have to look at our wonders, not focus on the blunders. **Peaceful partnership is achieved only by respecting each one's personal style unconditionally. Even though we can't change one another, we can still redesign the model if we need to do so.**

Innovative couples shed light on how to live inventively, not disruptively. They teach us to resolve love life dilemmas by not letting the past define present potential. Mystery remains more important than history. They sculpt solutions which fit their circumstances, not the rest of society's. Remember, only you and your lovemate can be the architects of these positive possibilities. Your shared visions provide the truest reading to chart your destination and destinies. Don't allow fear to stop you cold. Look over the edge and choose from the vast array of love style possibilities. Perhaps, you'll even devise one of your very own.

SHARED SPACE HASSLES

Several years ago, *USA Today* published revealing statistics on what bothers men and women most about living with another person. The article indicated that 40% of men and 35% of women found sloppiness the most irritating characteristic. Women were nearly twice as concerned about uneven sharing of chores, 32% to 15%. About one out of four men and women alike listed irritating personal habits as the most obnoxious aspect of shared living. Another 22% of men, but just 9% of women, had invasion of personal privacy at the top of their list.

We may laugh at such reports, but living together often heightens idiosyncrasies which can drive a wedge between lovemates. He doesn't clean the bathroom sink after shaving. She insists he only use certain towels. He leaves the bathroom floor all wet after a shower. He likes to exercise in the apartment. She doesn't like her living space turned into a gym. He likes to eat in bed. She'll only eat at the table. These examples of shared space hassles as well as poor roommate etiquette are the nit picky little things that wear on one's nerves. The list of all time favorite hassles is almost inexhaustible, and can also be a smoke screen for real relationship dissatisfactions.

Shared space hassles frequently escalate into divisive power struggles. Each spouse feigns a self-righteous posture around transporting the garbage, cleaning the bathroom, fixing the leaky faucet, cooking dinner, etc. This only serves to inflame hostilities which can soon dramatically shrink the perception of one's living area. An 8,000 square foot mansion can feel more like an 800 square foot apartment during an intense struggle. Conflict can also vastly expand the perception of emotional distance. Being in the same room with an adversarial spouse may be like standing on distant continents, the more distant the better.

STRESS FROM INTERNAL SCRIPTS

Not only do we experience stress from the "outside," we also must contend with stress on the "inside." Negative scripts like implanted cassette tapes rent space in our heads. Here's a generic list you probably can relate to. There's the pressure to perform sexually and have great sex. To go to church. To produce financially. To communicate truthfully. To keep in touch with friends and relatives. To have great sex. To call your mother. To remember birthdays and special occasions. To recycle. To be environmentally correct. To be politically correct. To be sexually correct. To buy your own home. To have a fulfilling job. To have kids. To be in shape. To do the right thing. To take exotic vacations. To own a beautiful car. To buy a bigger diamond. To have great sex. To join the country club. To be seen. To be attractive. To join the health club. To be brainy. To be brawny. To be busty. To be topical. To have perfect skin. To have great teeth. To be endowed where it counts. And finally, to buy the latest innovation, the skiswimwalksitjogrider, to have perfect abs and buns in order to have great sex. Enough already!

Wouldn't it be great if we could throw out those tapes that keep us from enjoying what we do have? Doubts about not being "good enough" haunt us with yearning for what lies just out of reach. Guilt trips, obsessions, "if onlys," unrealistic expectations, and Madison Avenue driven desires contribute to a state of perceived deprivation.

Who really cares if we don't have the fanciest car, most current wardrobe or near flawless diamond? Who really notices? We've been brainwashed to think we're supposed to care. If everyone drove their cars till they fell apart and wore the same clothes year in and year out, the economy would collapse. If it's not new, better, or more expensive, we just don't cut it. It's time to erase those tapes which don't serve us, and fast forward to those that do. What head tapes can you stop playing, so you can de-stress without further distress to yourself and your lovemate?

A WORD OF CAUTION

Though newer love styles enable many couples to live and love more comfortably, most of society is still somewhat less than accepting of those who don't mirror the marital mainstream. Unconventional lifestyles are perceived as somehow deviant, a threat to those who have their own fixed belief system of how everyone should cohabitate. For them, having intimacy with autonomy, commitment without control simply means someone is commitment phobic or destined for an affair. However, for the vast majority of inventively married and committed couples the reverse is patently true. They are religious, monogamous and adhere to every one of society's traditional values. They just happen to need or prefer an unconventional living style to make it all work.

Those who live more separately, such as having their own bedrooms are not just "playing house." Several bedrooms, or even two beds, can often enliven a waning sex life with the necessary space some individuals prefer. You, too, probably thought it was weird when you saw someone's parents with separate bedrooms. "My God, they must never have sex!" On the contrary, double beds or bedrooms frequently double your pleasure, provided they aren't a disguised form of withdrawal. **Time apart generally builds anticipation of time together for couples who still genuinely care about one another.** Commitment without control, paradoxically, curtails "wanderlust" infidelity when mature love prevails.

Perhaps the biggest mistake of any love life strategy is to oversell its virtues. Every approach has its limitations, and social architecture is no exception. Love styles must be flexible since our need of intimacy and autonomy typically varies throughout our lives. What's worked for many years, may eventually become impractical or unwanted.

In addition to all this, it cannot be overstated that reshaping one's love style is not going to rescue an essentially toxic relationship. To rethink a couple's time, space, and responsibilities does not magically transform spousal abuse into acts of genuine caring.

For spouses on the verge of divorce, love styles can at times instill hope, even save the day for some shaky marriages. Redesigns have usually been resorted to as a last ditch effort to reduce tensions and temporarily forestall divorce. However, when applied sooner or from the start, they can enhance a couple's chances for long term satisfaction. Naturally, there will always be those couples who, like children, blame each other for all life's problems. Divorce for them may be a **necessary** step to preserve the well being of all family members. There comes a time when such couples need to cut their losses, learn and move on. **In marriages where a husband and wife are already emotionally divorced without any signs of hope, different love styles should not be used to prolong the inevitable.** Social architecture does not pretend to be America's cure-all for its infidelity and divorce pandemic. It does, however, offer great promise as a largely unexplored potential antidote for many distressed couples for whom divorce is not the immediate answer or perhaps even necessary.

4 How Love Styles Arise

Changing strategy is far more caring than asking someone to stifle who they are in order to survive cohabitation. When mature love is flavored with the right recipe of space, time, and distance, the likelihood of "til death, not divorce, do us part" is greatly enhanced.

Throughout our lives, we periodically makeover our homes, appearance, etc. Why? Because every so often we just feel a need for change. A new hairstyle or outfit enables us to reinvent ourselves in some small, but significant way. No matter how much we liked it last year, we replace it the next. However, most of us can't afford to totally rearrange our faces, or buy a new home because we tire of the old one. We work with what we have, reupholster the couch, or refinish the kitchen cabinets. As far as appearances, we cut our hair short, grow a mustache, or become a blonde. In terms of a life partner though, why go fishing for someone else? Many times we already have the "right stuff" and just need to tweak things a bit to get moving again.

All too often, we unwittingly still expect relationships to remain unaltered forever. It was good enough for mom and dad so it's good enough for me. How realistic is this notion in the world we live in today or of the future? Perhaps, more than ever before, a rejuvenated relationship may at some point be appropriate, not a change of mate. To explore new love styles helps us see that our differences are just that, not reasons to abandon ship.

Unwanted togetherness eventually results in uncoupling. We need to focus on wanted togetherness which brings about recoupling. Renegotiating boundaries makes shared and alone time special, even sacred. To mutually choose the how, when and where of your togetherness is a powerful joining experience.

Inventive love styles give relationships
a chance for "elationship"

CREATIVE COMPROMISE

New love styles are born when both partners acknowledge their conflicts and open to unique solutions. Mary, 38, an advertising executive, and Ed, 53, a T.V. scriptwriter, choose to make things work despite or because of the 70 miles between them. Since neither wanted to relocate and leave their job, a win-win compromise gave them the best of both worlds. Each does their own thing during the week. They then spend Friday through Sunday together, taking turns at each location.

Ed's city apartment, with its many entertainment venues, and Mary's mountain retreat are an unbeatable combination. When separated they still feel connected because, as Mary puts it, "we're always working on mutual projects like ads and television shows. We constantly stimulate each other with ideas which generally peak on our weekend retreats. During the week, I have the complete solitude I need to translate these ideas into words. Everything considered, I'd say we have a very balanced and stimulating marriage. I adore it."

The following three couples unfortunately have not yet learned to get beyond their self-righteousness. Winning a power struggle means more to them than sharing a positive process or outcome. **Remember, lovemates become teammates only when they work together to defeat the problem, not one another.**

Joan and Stan

Joan and Stan are married six years. They adopted Jamie, their four year old daughter. At 48, Stan's business has taken off, which requires him to spend more time traveling. Although Joan is happy for him, she feels saddled with most of the household and child rearing chores. She'd rather start her own catering business, but has put the family's needs ahead of her own. Lately, arguments about who takes care of Jamie, takes the dog for a walk or runs an errand occur with alarming regularity. Stan ponders whether to put his business or family first. Regrettably he chooses more work on the road after only minimal discussion with Joan which sets up their power struggle.

Creative compromise might involve taking some of Stan's added income to pay for a sitter and maid service to free Joan from her responsibilities. Stan might even hire a part-time assistant to travel in his place on occasion, so he can see his family more. Joan could work several hours weekly for an established caterer to see what it was like. **Alternatives become evident only when both persons decide they would rather stay together than make each other wrong.**

David and Elise

After three years, David and Elise have a year old daughter, Joy. David has a high stress job with a securities firm on Wall Street. Elise has returned to finish medical school after a leave of absence. Though they have a nanny during the day, David finds it difficult to share in nightly childcare. He continually assumes Elise will handle these duties. Elise is fuming inside since she's made it clear that her career does not take a back seat to David's. She's just as tired as he is when they relieve the nanny at night. David and Elise share progressively divisive conflict where neither wants to budge. Like children playing tug of war, their continuous win-lose struggle for supremacy drains off what little energy is left for family life. **Any win-lose becomes lose-lose, where future retaliations even the score. Ultimately, nobody wins in a power struggle but the attorneys.**

For creative compromise, David and Elise could elect to share some childcare activities such as giving baths, telling bedtime stories, etc. These soon could become times for family fun and bonding. Another compromise might be to take turns as primary parent every few nights. They might reward themselves by retaining the nanny's services on selected evenings or weekends so **they** can go out and play. Couples have just so much energy available to either heighten a conflict or resolve it. It's a conscious choice. Sadly, there are too many couples who have little else except their conflicts to hold them together. **They share an attachment, not a relationship.**

John and Susan

It's been a two year run for John and Susan's committed pairing. Before moving in together three months ago they never realized just how disjointed their daily living styles could be. As a professional writer, John spends entire days in bed writing, while Susan feels the bedroom should be off limits with regard to work. Since the bedroom was more "his" than "theirs," Susan felt displaced in her new home.

One creative compromise called for John and Susan to have two beds or two bedrooms. This way John could continue his work comfortably, while Susan no longer felt like an orphan in her own house. Another suggestion was to create an office in the house where John felt "comfy" and inspired to write. It could even be designed around a futon. This way the bedroom is kept as a sensual space for Susan while John's needs are also met.

During a couple's conflict,
the last thing they want to do is let go of their leverage,
which is exactly what needs to happen first

Creative compromise enables each partner to come out a winner. This is essential to all kinds of shared space challenges. Partners who differ as early morning or late night people, snorers and non-snorers, restless and sound sleepers, plus those who wish to display hobbies, do better with their own bedrooms or hobby rooms. Instead of wrestling over the remote, separate sets with earplugs, or different T.V. rooms minimize viewing tussles. This way she can see "the game" on ESPN and he can watch the Home Shopping Network. What's wrong with this picture? **According to marital research, how well spouses resolve conflicts in a mutually respectful manner is the #1 predictor of long term marital satisfaction, over and above every other factor.**

As individuals evolve, their love styles need to keep pace. When we put on a few pounds, either our clothes have to be let out or we have to buy new ones. Otherwise, we are uncomfortable. Wearing a larger size temporarily solves the problem, but we still need to watch what we eat, exercise, etc. **Even with clear communication there will always be times when two people are out of sync. Just acknowledging the Double Downer, or DUD effect, and lowering expectations helps keep negative energy from escalating into useless power struggles.** Whenever partners are kept in the dark about one's changing concerns, there is only the illusion of harmony. While relatively simple redesigns help balance out relationships, bigger picture issues must always be kept in mind, and when necessary, brought to the table.

LOVE STYLES ARISE FROM CRISIS

Various love styles are usually created in response to ongoing love life challenges. Any crisis which threatens the stability of a marriage presents an exciting opportunity for a "marriage makeover." Crises such as an out of state job prospect, a spouse's desire to return to school, children leaving the nest, illnesses, and so forth can lead to either a more functional love style or major social upheaval.

Often, to diffuse tensions and avert a divorce, couples separate. Most of those who stay separated for six months or longer eventually divorce. Spouses who separate for only a few months and then return, usually continue in the marriage. However, there arc also a few spouses who pursue a third option, continuing both the marriage and separate residences. **It is this last group who use the crisis of separation as an unintended opportunity to form a more functional love style for their marriage.**

Another fortuitous love style occurs when divorcees marry again, but keep some degree of autonomy. He moves into his new wife's home, but since furniture styles clash, his possessions are relocated in the attic. Events unfold which eventually lead to his own attic apartment and a "Bi-Level Marriage." They also retain their own last names, bank accounts and credit cards, with a shared household account for joint expenses. As you can see, new love styles are often created by happenstance during major personal transitions.

Nonetheless, there are a few couples who know beforehand that living together would be like an El Niño winter blast. They are not particularly gun shy, like many who've been burned by a prior divorce. They simply realize their clashes in neatness, decor, personal habits or temperament make them unsuitable as conventional house mates. However, they have the foresighted courage to start a Neighborhood Marriage, living within the same housing complex or at least nearby. The design works especially well for children, with mom and dad only a few minutes walk away. These are rare couples, but they do exist. **While state of the art love styles look very much like a divorce to the casual observer, they may actually pave the way for a better marriage.**

A marriage makeover can also occur when one or both spouses work out of town 40% to 50% of the time. Neither feels inclined to sacrifice their career goals. Sometimes **Time Share Spouses** even rendezvous at airport hotels for romantic refuelings. This builds anticipation while deepening their trust on the road. Home reunions also help release pent up passions. Of course, if both spouses travel in their chosen professions, children are not a viable option until someone decides to stay home.

In past decades, 50's wives rarely ever had mobile careers except as airline stewardesses. Even then, the wife usually deferred to her husband's career and played Susie Homemaker. In the 90's, many female executives routinely travel out of town on business trips. They don't subserviently give up a rewarding profession because of a husband's itinerant career.

DUAL CAREER MARRIAGE MAKEOVERS

Everyday, the media bombard us with news of social casualties. United States Census Bureau figures declare that nearly one third of women ages 35 to 39 have already divorced. We are also informed that 60% of women who marry in their thirties can expect to divorce in their lifetime. About 40% of them will not remarry, according to the National Center for Health Statistics. For those women who divorce in their forties, seven out of ten will also never remarry. Such findings are in part influenced by career minded women, those who earn more than $30,000 per year and divorce at a rate 4 times higher than lower salaried females. Earning capacity and marketability provide them a passport out of dead-end marriages. In the 90's, wives file for divorce almost 70% of the time.

Dual career couples now comprise about 80% of American marriages. In 20% of dual career households, wives now earn higher salaries than their husbands. A new breed of House Husband also stays home with pre-school age children. Mr. Mom does the grocery shopping, meal preparation and laundry. Mrs. Exec. brings home the bacon. Today's role reversals, while at times wreaking havoc in the boardroom and bedroom, also create an emerging mutual respect for what it's like to walk in the other's moccasins.

A fascinating spin off of Mr. Mom Marriages is when a husband follows his wife's career move to another city. In the 50's, women certainly had jobs. However, not too many had careers, especially ones which required them to move cross-country for advancement. Wives in the 90's frequently make career moves, while their husbands stay back with the kids to finish out school and get the house ready for sale. It's not unusual today for such spouses and children to remain geographically separated for up to six months or even longer. Federal government and corporate employees are particularly susceptible to such geographic relocations. Contemporary spouses are forced to juggle family priorities with career aspirations in order to remain a family unit and still move up the corporate staircase.

Advantages of New Love Styles

New love styles can virtually eliminate many of the conflicts shared space hassles pose for contemporary couples. For example, in Bi-Level Marriages husbands and wives live on different levels of the same house. They may have their own entertainment centers, kitchens, bathrooms, and bedrooms, which offer them the privacy they prefer. Responsibility for their own laundry, groceries, checking accounts and cleaning is like performing marital bypass surgery, with most blame games removed. **The chore wars no longer have to be waged.**

By now, some of you are probably asking, "whatever happened to good old 'working things out' in marriage?" Simply put, peoples' lives today are so complex that there needs to be a much greater variety of ways to work things out. You and your beloved are blessed if you both are compatible and mature enough to live together in a conventional household. Unfortunately, not everyone is. Sometimes it becomes necessary to remove the combatants from their stockpile of weapons, so vertical or horizontal positioning of the toilet seat becomes a moot point once and for all.

Shared space hassles are greatly minimized by love style variations, since couples are no longer squeezed together like sardines. When a couple shifts from one residential design to another they qualify as a **Modular Marriage**. At various life phases, they may be Traditional Spouses, a Condo Couple, Duplex Spouses, or have Sidekick Apartments. **Such couples often enjoy more quality time living apart than when they lived together under one roof, sharing the same bed.**

For those convinced residential redesigns are too expensive, check out the financial and emotional costs of any contested divorce. At least this way each person can still own their own tax sheltered property, which typically beats a long term treasury note any day. Otherwise, in many divorce scenarios neither spouse winds up owning any property since it has to be sold. Proceeds are mostly squandered among attorneys, real estate agents, closing costs and Uncle Sam. Ex-spouses keep what's left, which usually isn't enough to buy another dwelling, at least the one they want. With Dual Location Marriages, spouses can still own their residences, partly as a financial hedge if the marriage ever does wind up on a dead end street.

Statistics claim the majority of all divorces in the United States occur among persons 25 to 54 years of age. Spouses 55 years and older, who consummate later life marriages, prove much more true to the vow "til death do us part." Remarkably, 90% of those who marry in later life, live out their years without resorting to divorce. **Perhaps they've learned to compromise, without compromising themselves.** It is intriguing how older couples eventually learn to live in relative harmony. A cynic might conclude that they merely settle for what they have, and give up on attracting a more desirable or younger spouse. Nevertheless, companionship should never be underrated, especially with someone who shares a similar historical and age perspective. Being born from the same era provides a comforting sort of "generation glue" which binds older spouses together. These remain merely provocative speculations until someone researches what makes later life marriages really tick so well.

COUPLES LIVING WITH LIFESTYLE DIFFERENCES

Spouses who either both smoke, or don't, are today's rule of thumb. However, what happens when a wife who has smoked throughout a marriage stops, and her husband still wants to continue his three pack a day habit? Should they divorce? This nicotine challenged marriage might survive with its own designated smoking area. **If necessary, however, a nicotine addicted spouse might have to move into a private apartment, so the marriage does not go up in flames.**

Lifestyle divorces where there are irreconcilable health concerns are becoming much more commonplace. How many couples have paid the ultimate price for drawing a line in the sand, when they might have redesigned the sandbox and continued to play? One woman withheld all forms of affection from her smoking husband to get him to quit. Now she's burning emotionally, still waiting after four months to share a hug. **Most lifestyle differences over health issues can be mitigated, provided a husband and wife choose not to make themselves sick about it.**

As time marches on, dual residences or living quarters within the same environment will become just as mundane as twin beds are today. In addition, it will be unusual if at least one spouse doesn't live and work at home. **The Stay-At-Home Dual Career Couple** will be your friends, neighbors, or even yourselves. **Marital metamorphosis, not rigor mortis, must take place in order for our most essential institution to survive as society's primary building block.**

5 Love Styles of Twelve Creative Couples

These twelve couples were interviewed to learn how love style redesigns helped them surmount time, space, and role conflicts. Their redesigns focus on resolving issues, not perpetuating them, with a conscious emphasis on strengths. The marriage was elevated above either spouse's personal priority to be right. This shift to a mutual problem solving mode enables obstacles once considered insurmountable to be reframed and resolved. Let's see how these inventive married couples did it, often without the support of family, friends, or society.

SAME RESIDENCE REDESIGNS

SAME RESIDENCE REDESIGN #1
Separate Bedrooms

Mary and Hank
Redesign for Passionate Sex and Restful Sleep

Mary and Hank each lived through painful first marriages and divorces. Mary has a four year old son, Tommy. They remarried three years ago. Mary recalls, "I wasn't sleeping well. Hank is a restless sleeper who tosses and turns all night. I wanted to toss him right out of bed."

They also spent the past several winters reinfecting each other with the flu bug, which made rest and recovery almost impossible. What concerned them even more was their waning desire as lovers. Hank remembers how they even refrained from cuddling. Each became an extension of the bed, like an extra pillow. Instead of making love, sex became a reliable sleep aid, like a glass of warm milk, but without the cookie. Passion was a faded memory, with Tommy the sole outlet for their pent up affection.

During love style coaching, they experimented with the "radical" notion of separate bedrooms. Within a month, passion was alive and well again. Touching and cuddling were once more a daily occurrence. Lovemaking triumphed over sleeping pill sex. The big question now was "your bedroom or mine?" With Tommy fast asleep, the rest of the house opened up for more spontaneous "Mary making." **Historically, separate bedrooms has signaled a sexual "stale" mate.** However, this new love style served as a springboard for sexual renewal, with more restful sleep supplying the energy.

SAME RESIDENCE REDESIGN #2
Time Share Bi-Level Marriage
(Main Floor-Basement)

Janice and Clark
Redesign for Intimacy with Autonomy

Janice and Clark have their own version of a Time Share Marriage. They were each divorced and quite comfortable as singles. They both hoped for a closer marriage the second time around, but not too close. Like other time share couples, Janice and Clark are apart about half their lives. Clark travels extensively as regional sales manager for a Fortune 500 company. Janice heads a busy insurance agency. Each feels exhausted and exhilarated by their independent lifestyles. Janice and her ten year old daughter, Melody, live on the main floor of Janice's ranch style home in suburban

Denver. Clark, divorced after 23 years, with one grown son, has his own basement apartment in Janice's house.

Their Bi-Level Marriage was developed more by accident than any specific plan. After they married, Janice ran short of closet space when Clark moved into her house. He began to store his belongings in the basement. Gradually he started using the lower level as his private living space. Her furniture was Early American and his Early Goodwill which necessitated separate quarters even more. "We eat most meals upstairs which Clark visits whenever he likes," Janice explained. Usually Melody and Janice don't visit the basement. "It's really wonderful in the winter on a snowy day," quipped Janice. "He does his thing down in his apartment while I'm upstairs doing mine. It's like living in our own homes without the drive time."

Since inquiring minds want to know...yes, they usually make love upstairs. Since Clark is an insomniac, he'll often leave Janice's bed for his apartment in the wee morning hours to work crossword puzzles or watch television. Clark is also a chronic smoker and only lights up on his turf. They've also chosen to keep original names, separate bank accounts and investments. Household bills get split right down the middle.

"People have various reactions to us," Janice chuckled. "They want to fix us and predict once we learn to trust each other...we'll share our money, live together and have a real marriage." One incensed associate of Janice's insisted they had nothing that could be considered "ours." As far as she was concerned, and she was very concerned, they had nothing more than a "pseudo marriage." Friends, however, have applauded them for doing whatever it takes to prolong lust and love. Janice and Clark clearly adore both their time together and apart.

Historically, Time Share Marriages have been around ever since men have pursued their favorite pastime of world conquest. More contemporary versions of the conqueror include traveling salesman, politician, truck driver, pilot and the still popular soldier boy. Nowadays, both spouses may have military or civilian careers which take them all over the globe. Women currently comprise 25% of this country's military. Without question, Time Share Marriages represent 21st Century relationship reality, where courtship can be extended indefinitely based upon anticipation of both loving departures and reunions.

SAME RESIDENCE REDESIGN #3
Bi-level Marriage
(Attic-Basement with Shared Common Space)

Tim and Alice
Redesign for Creative Living

Tim and Alice are both creative types, artist and aspiring romance novelist respectively. Married three years, they plan to wait another year before starting a family. Over time, each felt more and more trapped by their 1,200 square foot dwelling. Resentment mounted as each invaded the other's creative space. Alice scapegoated Tim for her bouts of writer's block, while Tim returned the favor for his own episodes of artist's block.

Just as we consult an interior designer about a home's style statement, Tim and Alice arrived at several marital redesigns through love style coaching. First they sold their little gingerbread house and purchased a three story townhouse. While Tim devised a studio for the attic, Alice was in "Wonderland" with her own writer's study in the finished basement. Each enjoyed their new creative distance and work spaces. They frequently met for lunch dates at noon in the kitchen, or took each other out. Afternoon delight means dessert is served at home with lots of affectionate confections. According to Tim, "the creative juices are definitely starting to flow again."

SAME RESIDENCE REDESIGN #4
Duplex Marriage with Two Self Contained Living Units

Pat and John
Redesign for Stepfamily Marriage

Like countless "blended" families, this Stepfamily Marriage soon became another Brady Bunch run amuck. The four children, ranging in age from 11 to 14, became instant adversaries fighting for all the undivided love and territory they could get. One time, John's sons actually duct taped Pat's daughters in their bedroom. Both parents spent two hellish years trying to live out the myth of one big happy family. Finally, burned out and on the brink of divorce, John moved himself and his sons into an apartment several blocks away.

Although everyone enjoyed the relative calm, John and Pat lost continuity as husband and wife. Pat worked late hours as a real estate agent, while John spent many long hours at his law practice. Time away became greater than times together. After eight frustrating months they were both ready to file divorce papers. Miraculously, the crisis inspired John to try one last gasp measure. He got a zoning variance to renovate a newly built single family dwelling into a duplex. This architectural redesign included completely separate entrances, living quarters, kitchens and laundry rooms. John also built in a connecting master bedroom for himself and Pat.

They now saw each other every day and night while mealtimes were spent with their own brood. Once a month they all came perfunctorily together for dinner. Pat reflected, "it worked out great for us and literally saved our marriage." Some friends were skeptical at first, even strangely threatened by their success. They felt the Browns used an architectural Band-Aid instead of family therapy to fix their real problems. Several therapists who heard about it, thought the parents had completely copped out, despite seven fruitful duplex marriage years. On the other hand, John and Pat and the children felt they **had** worked through many family issues, just not in the way traditional therapists recommend.

When all the children left the nest, the Browns sold the "duplex" after retrofitting it as a single family dwelling. Ironically, Pat's daughters and John's sons have become good friends. Today they hold very poignant family gatherings during the holidays, when the entire clan assembles as one family. The Browns feel this happened once they were no longer forced to share their parents and living space. Pat and John have since moved into their own home with only one kitchen and one living room. Now their only break with tradition is use of a second backup bedroom on an as needed basis. This became necessary since both are promiscuous snorers and generally thrash about during the night. When snoring cannot be managed by any other means, the Browns advocate that couples employ this "snore room" strategy even if just a living room is available.

Perhaps in the next century, Duplex Marriage Designed Homes with separate and shared living space will become more mainstream in the construction industry. With 27 million stepfamilies, according to the U.S. Population Reference Bureau, there certainly is a sizeable enough market to make it commercially feasible,. One can envision someday, an entire housing division of Duplex Marriage Designed Homes with a variety of socially architected floor plans from which to choose. Sorry, duct tape not included.

SAME RESIDENCE REDESIGN #5
Individualized Living within a Shared Household

Jim and Anita
Redesign for Intentional Togetherness

It's been 28 years and three grown children later for the Fields. Jim is an inventor, while Anita works as a design engineer. Jim rarely feels jealous of his wife's extensive travels with male colleagues. He travels widely as well in his entrepreneurial efforts to test market his products.

Remarkably, Jim and Anita designed their lives for intentional togetherness from the start. They built their home from day one with the intention of sleeping in separate bedrooms. Jim prefers an incredibly firm sleeping surface, whereas Anita must have a very soft sleep cushion. Jim feels comfortable with his bedroom temperature at 58 degrees. Anita, as you probably guessed, likes to have her thermostat right around 80. Of course, they make love in the living room common space at a negotiated 70 degrees. Besides separate and shared living areas, the Fields designed adjacent dens with a see through connecting fireplace. Since each enjoys entirely different television shows, music and books, they only visit the other's den when they can occasionally agree upon a particular movie rental.

Anita and Jim have socially designed for the future as well. They've placed several small bedrooms downstairs so their adult children can bring the grandkids overnight. However, the bedrooms are purposely cramped and poorly furnished, "so they won't stay too long." Anita admits she prefers no more than two or three day visits at a time.

Jim has also designed another downstairs living unit for the time when they "get old and need help." He feels a healthcare professional could live there as needed. They hope to avoid ever moving into a nursing home and see home healthcare as much more cost effective. This visionary couple has socially architected for both present autonomy and future dependency. They plan to share intentional togetherness until death do they part and no doubt beyond. Next, we shift from love style redesigns for the same residence to those with different addresses.

SEPARATE RESIDENCE REDESIGNS

SEPARATE RESIDENCE REDESIGN #1
Crosstown Weekend Marriage

Arlene and Jeff
Redesign for Geographically Distant Careers

In their nine year marriage, Arlene and Jeff have been blessed with two sons, now three and four years old. Arlene is Doctor of Obstetrics and Associate Professor at a New York City medical school. Jeff has his Ph.D. in Reproductive Endocrinology and is Associate Professor at the same medical school. They live as do many contemporary dual career families, with the preschoolers in daycare during the week.

Unexpectedly, Jeff was offered a once in a lifetime department head position at a very prestigious medical school in another county. To commute was just not practical so they quickly reached an impasse. Jeff accepted the position with mixed emotion. Without a plan in mind, he rented a crosstown apartment close to his new job. Like a rabbit out of the hat, their Crosstown Marriage burst upon the scene.

They began seeing each other on weekends, but when a judgmental friend thought Arlene was shortchanging herself and the kids, she had to respond. Arlene said to her, "in my work I see all kinds of women who assume they're happily married, but I know most hookers aren't kept busy by single 40 year old lawyers. They're employed by these womens' husbands on 'monkey' business trips. The interesting thing about our kids is they have no preconceptions what a family is supposed to be like. Our children have adapted very well. I keep waiting, but they seem very happy and secure."

Arlene clarified, "Our jobs are demanding and far apart. The commute would be terrible. I know a lot of kids whose fathers leave home at 6 a.m. and return when the children are asleep. Commuter dads don't see their kids until the weekend anyway, which is all Jeff does." She reminded her friend, "Couples grow apart or have extramarital affairs whether they live together or not. Women cry in my office how their husbands don't contribute anything besides dirty laundry. Many men are already Wally World weekend dads. Jeff, the kids and I make quality weekends happen. We love to cuddle in bed with the boys. Our times together have become even more precious than ever." Arlene added, "I look around at all the single moms and ask myself one question, 'what really is destructive to children?' I feel the real problem is all the angry, bitter feelings between parents, not divorce itself or who lives where. I'm astounded at just how judgmental and threatened others get about our Crosstown Marriage. It works well for us, but we're not imposing it on anyone. My advice to other couples is to each their own."

In any example of Crosstown Marriage, **home is where the hearts are, not just the bodies.** Today's dual career couples appear more receptive to each other's crosstown, cross state or out of state education and careers.

Finally, Jeff shared his own personal reflections. "Mature love transcends all distance. I don't need to live in the same home to securely love my wife and children. If a person must always be in the same place as their partner to feel loved, they are immature and so is their love."

SEPARATE RESIDENCE REDESIGN #2
Rotating Parenthood Apartment Marriage

Ted and Jackie
Redesign for Parenthood Relief

Ted and Jackie have been a dual career couple for seven years. The Charles' children Jon, age six, and Marcia, almost five, are very bright and active. Over the years this couple has completely burned out on their roles as mommy and daddy. Each has lost a sense of who they are, where family commitment has turned into confinement.

For burned out parents, monogamy often becomes monotony as well. Family autopsies of similar couples reveal parents who no longer feel alive, often overeat and overspend. They stop taking care of themselves, the house, and the children. In a very real sense they rebel against their roles and each other. Depression sets in. They want someone to take care of them. Daily hassles build until the marriage is bankrupt, only to become another one of society's disposables. However, burned out parents don't generally want divorce as much as they need relief.

Instead of seeing an attorney, Jackie consulted love style coaching. In several weeks, with the help of an apartment locator service, she found an apartment and signed a month to month lease. After she moved some of her clothes and furniture into the apartment, she entertained a few of her women friends. Jackie began to feel like her old self again while she stayed in touch with Ted and the kids. Within a month, Jackie's transformation was obvious to friends, the children, Ted and most especially herself. Imagine, all this without Prozac. What a concept!

While Jackie originally considered a trial separation, love style coaching helped her and Ted negotiate a novel Separate Residence Redesign. The first two weeks of the month, Jackie lived in the apartment while Ted parented the kids. The next two weeks they rotated residences again, but this time Jackie returns home as primary parent, while Ted becomes the apartment dweller.

Now they frequently hire a sitter so they can romance each other all over again and have their own "extra" marital relationship at the apartment. Each feels supported to be the person they were before. No longer are they inmates in parental prison. Time shared parenting and dual residences have freed Jackie and Ted to give the kids their best, and appreciate the magic of childhood. Remarkably, they now share more family activities, day trips and vacations than when they lived as one big frenzied family. What do the neighbors have to say about all this? Not too much, especially since several recently became the community's first Condo Couple.

SEPARATE RESIDENCE REDESIGN #3
Condo Couple

Betty and Robert
Redesign for Intimacy with Independence

The popularity of townhouses and condominiums has made independent living affordable for millions of Americans. Many previously married or never married singles can enjoy their own living quarters without the more expensive responsibility of private home ownership. This has provided couples, married or not, a ready-made opportunity to live in adjacent or nearby condos and townhouses. While condo couples usually meet by chance, some have actually planned to rent or purchase condos in close proximity.

One real life example is 38 year old Betty, and Robert who is 40, both professional educators. Robert has legal and physical custody of Allen, his thirteen year old Nintendo whiz kid. They live in a large condo complex in Baltimore. Betty, also divorced, has no whiz kids. She is determined to have a better relationship than she had in her marriage. Robert and Betty have come to love each other very much during a two year commitment, but still fear losing everything again through another marriage and divorce.

Their redesign of nearby condos fell into their laps when Robert's neighbor and best pal, Pete, was transferred to Chicago. He offered Betty his condo at a great price. When she decided to buy it and stop renting, the idea to become a Condo Couple was born. Robert can now visit Betty without need of a sitter for Allen. Since their condos are within several minutes walk, Robert has, on occasion, spent the entire night at Betty's. Allen feels perfectly safe with Betty's phone number tucked under his pillow. He is proud his dad can trust him to take care of himself.

Living separately has also kept parenting roles very clear for everyone. These, of course, frequently become blurred for live-in couples and stepfamilies. Living so close helps them to open their hearts once again, without shared space hassles, or fear of painful exit logistics if they should ever break up. This redesign could continue to work for them indefinitely. However, in the future it is quite feasible they might get married. They have enjoyed taking turns spending up to two or three days together at each other's home, with Allen joining them part of the time. When Allen moves out, they might even sell off one of the condos and live together.

SEPARATE RESIDENCE REDESIGN #4
His and Her Apartments

Adele and John
Redesign for Different Living Styles

Some years ago, a fascinating article appeared in *House and Garden Magazine* entitled, "A Playwright's Style." In it, John Guare and Adele Chatfield-Taylor described their adjoining His and Her Apartment Marriage in an old Greenwich Village apartment building. Thanks to building codes, an eight foot wide service hall became the architectural equivalent of a marital buffer zone. They came to think of it as "the secret to happy marriage or even life itself."

Playwright Guare was characterized as "hopelessly messy," and his wife, Adele, as "impeccably neat." She explained, "I like home to be soothing while John likes home to be entertaining." Adele drew the analogy of John's world as "a three-ring circus," hers, a "reflecting pool." Adele immaculately arranged Hermes scarves and jewelry on her French bed in contrast to John's controlled chaos of scattered books, papers and clothes.

What John and Adele found so interesting was **their differences stemmed more out of form than substance.** They both prized punctuality, enjoyed cats, dogs, reading and much more. Even John's Victorian style furniture and Adele's traditional furnishings were not all that dissimilar, just the way each chose to "organize the stuff." John liked to work at home with "books, looseleaf pages and notebooks, detective stories, Bic pens, rolls of Scotch tape, a hole punch, scissors, staples, the *New York Times*, mail, his Rolodex, the telephone and his dogs all in bed with him while creating a project." John's almost Zen like practice allowed, "everything to stay exactly where it was, sometimes for years at a time." ·

Living as they did in Sidekick Apartments disturbed many of their friends, including Adele's mother, who wanted them to "knock out the walls." Adele informed her mother she was not going to move in with her new husband and "let a little matter such as old fashioned matrimony ruin a good thing." Certainly not all married couples who share very different living styles like John and Adele, can afford such a solution. However, when one factors in all the costs of divorce, both legal and emotional, one wonders in the long run which social architectural choice is most frugal? After all, somehow individuals manage to pay for their own living spaces before meeting and becoming a couple. Why not afterwards?

We can only speculate how many conventionally married Johns and Adeles have made their lives a living hell of broken dishes and dreams, when they might otherwise have flourished as Apartment Sidekicks. Several things can be said about the distinction between Apartment Sidekicks who rent, and Condo Couples who generally buy their living units. While more affluent couples are able to purchase their own residence, the concept of separate places is still quite feasible for couples who need or want to rent. Of course, one partner may own while the other rents. **Indeed, His and Hers might eventually be the least costly, practical alternative for Mr. and Mrs. in the next century.**

REDESIGN FOR MONEY MANAGEMENT

ROLE REDESIGN
Money Management

Marti and Jeff
Redesign for Cash Flow

Marti and Jeff have been husband and wife for six years. They entered marriage as the formal celebration of a four year committed relationship. Children, however, are not a priority. Marti makes very few decisions without considering her husband, who sorts mail for the U.S. Postal Service. "If it's a fancy lunch somewhere and Jeff isn't involved, I feel it takes away from our income. Is it fair to Jeff if I get to go somewhere nice, and he has to eat at a hamburger stand?" Marti works part-time as an elementary school substitute teacher.

When it comes to money, everything goes into one checking and one savings account. Each withdraws an allowance, which is called "mad money," according to Marti. They've tried separate checking accounts, but it was difficult for Jeff to keep up with it. He'd say, "just give me the cash." Marti manages their money flow now as household accountant.

"I take out the garbage, she does the books. Why not?" asks Jeff. Marti keeps Jeff posted on bills and funds available so he stays current. Jeff rarely pays by check, mainly using credit cards. "I sign all checks because I'm the one who keeps the checkbook," confirms Marti. Jeff quickly added, "but I do our taxes." Marti conceded, "I have a mental block doing our personal taxes for the IRS." She compliments Jeff on tracking all their yearly expenditures. Jeff expressed how secure he feels with his wife's money management during the year, which makes tax time a breeze.

For their mad money, each receives $100 monthly. "I don't know how he spends it, I don't care how he spends it," declared Marti. What inspired mad money was that when Jeff wanted to buy Marti a gift, he couldn't keep it secret because it showed up in their joint checking account. For Christmas and birthdays, both draw an extra $100. "Here, go spend a hundred bucks on me," Marti tells Jeff. Since their birthdays are in the same month, it's a convenient way to keep a secret. "We really like to buy each other gifts. We indulge each other as a prerequisite of our marriage," Jeff teased.

Marti and Jeff may not be typical of today's married money managers. They have virtually eliminated money hassles with a simple money flow and dispersal. Mutual indulgence, even in moderation, sets their standard. They surrender and share financial control, so loving energy is not diverted into money struggles.

REDESIGN FOR OTHER SEX FRIENDSHIP
Personal Friends Redesign

Peggy and Jim
Redesign for Female/Male Friendship

Five years ago Peggy and Jim Owens officially tied the knot. Each is now 29 years old. They have a mutual single friend, Joan. Peggy and Joan met as new hires for an international cosmetics firm. As regional sales manager, Peggy makes frequent out of town business trips. Jim's a city bus driver who Peggy feels needs to go out more and do things with Joan, when Peggy travels, because he gets lonely. "I'll be away for a few weeks at a time, so I generally encourage it, since she's our dear friend. People find this very weird. I totally trust them both, so I don't feel any big jealousy. Usually Jim goes out to a movie or to dinner with Joan," Peggy proudly proclaimed.

Peggy recalled a time early in their marriage when Jim was transferred to Denver for a promising sales position. She continued to stay at her marketing job in Houston for five more months. Peggy remembers her friend, Steve, taking her to dinner since he knew she was staying alone. Steve's voice carried quite loudly while standing in line to be seated. He blared out, "I've never been out with a married woman before." Peggy quipped, "Just about everyone in the restaurant looked over at us, so I shouted, 'It's not as exciting as it sounds folks. Bon Appetit!'"

The Owens' friends are mostly married now, but back in their early twenties, they had lots of single friends. They often did things with a friend as a trio, or one of them would share an activity with a friend of the opposite sex. Love styles which allow for such friendships usually threaten most couples. Nonetheless, we never outgrow our need for social contact whether it be with the same or other sex. Every couple must decide how to handle this sensitive issue.

From a love style perspective, jealousy is really no more than a Present Time Fear of a Future Time Loss, whereas fear is a Fantasy Experienced As Reality. **Jealousy usually is a form of control rather than a tribute to love.** Discomfort zones a couple needs to clarify include flirting, affection, hugs, kisses and social activities. Proper attention to personal boundaries from the start, heads off disruptive mistrust games down the road.

Many people struggle with fears of engulfment or losing themselves in their intimate relationships. Others want to lose themselves and get enmeshed. People may also control or distance out of fears of abandonment. Residential redesigns set boundaries creative couples feel are necessary for their interpersonal comfort and continuing love. Everyone tackles this emotional balancing act whenever we get seriously involved. However, even with the best therapy in the world, some of us just do better setting more finite boundaries. This helps many of us to feel more secure and less frightened so we can fulfill our potential as a love life partner.

The twelve pioneering couples interviewed, relied on their own survival instincts and ingenuity to manifest their personalized love styles. They traded in the old "Marital Rules Book" which set out what they were supposed to do, for what truly best fit their lives. Traditional marital values, however, were never compromised or redesigned in any way, nor should they ever be. Hopefully, this cornucopia of love style options inspires us to go that extra mile from the start, or at least before calling it quits when the fat lady does her thing.

6 The Ultimate Marriage Makeover

This particular marriage makeover is the most fascinating love style to date. The Heads, Marian and Glenn, and Hoags, Gail and Gregory, are two **monogamously married couples in their forties, who choose to live as one family under one roof.** They have lived communally now for more than 13 years. When I visited, they were living in their third house, a 6,000 square foot retreat surrounded by spruce trees, wildlife and the majestic Rocky Mountains. The house was purchased with all four names appearing on the joint tenancy title. Their story has more fateful twists and turns than Disneyland's Space Mountain, with important implications for the future of marriage and families.

How Both Couples Met, Married and Merged

Marian and Glenn met in 1981 at a professional association conference. She was staring at his picture on the wall, when Glenn introduced himself, and intuitively decided to hire her on the spot to do computer consulting for him. At first their relationship was strictly business. Marian was still married, working out of her Washington D.C. home, while Glenn lived in Denver, Colorado. His two children from a previous marriage lived with their mother.

Prior to their divorce, Marian's husband Avram also met Glenn, which led to another business partnership. They stayed with each other's families whenever they traveled east or west. After Marian divorced, Avram moved into Glenn's new house in Boulder, Colorado. During the next year, Glenn and Marian began a long distance romance. Marian had no desire to marry again, while Glenn did. They spent an entire week exploring what marriage really meant to both of them. Marian discovered they could have a much more spontaneous, joyful relationship than in her marriage. **She explained, "we didn't need to make any formal commitment at the time, instead we just discovered we were committed."**

Several months after Avram arrived, Gail also moved into Glenn's house. This happened when she and Glenn were introduced by Marian at Gail's sister's wedding. Gail was living in New York City at the time. She and Marian had been life-time friends, but had not seen each other for years.

They invited Gail to Colorado to ski, and by the end of her vacation Gail planned to move there. Glenn suggested Gail stay at the house with himself and Avram, just to help her relocate from New York. Marian was delighted with this arrangement. If things progressed with Glenn, she too would move to Boulder with her new sweetheart and her best friend both in the same house. A year and a half later, Marian and Glenn married, and Marian made her permanent move to Boulder in June of 1985. Avram was graciously dismissed from the household, while Gail was asked to stay on as care-taker, since Glenn and Marian were still frequent business flyers.

Several months after Marian moved in, Gail met Gregory. She was storing her art work in his garage, though they had never met. He carried her business card in his wallet for nine months after a friend had suggested they should meet. At first glance, they saw a future together.

Within a month, Gregory also moved into the house. He did, however, exercise "infinite" patience by waiting an entire week before proposing. Gail would not be stampeded into such an important decision and waited a full 20 seconds before granting her acceptance.

THE TWO FAMILY MARRIAGE

The Hoags were married, and the Heads stopped traveling. They now questioned whether they should all continue to live communally, or split into separate households. They pursued both options, looking for houses to share, or for just one couple. They soon discovered the larger homes they really liked were only affordable by both couples. **It made dollars and sense to pool all financial resources, and live happily ever after in the house of their collective dreams.**

The Heads' and Hoags' family marriage has worked because they know how to truly communicate. Issues are never left to fester. Both couples are very sensitive about how they handle shared space hassles and concerns of all kinds. Most marriages have their share of challenges. Just imagine, if you dare, what it might be like for you and your spouse to live with another married couple as part of a larger family. In this "marital twilight zone" you would be conspicuously different from all other marriages in the civilized world.

CREATIVE TOGETHERNESS FAMILY STYLE

When they all moved in together, there were no published guidelines for this virtual family reality. Each of them gravitated to the chores they liked to do. Being responsible, each adopted the philosophy of, "do a little bit more than 100%." A psychologist who briefly visited, suggested they ask each other such questions as, "how can we be better housemates?" They soon discovered weekly meetings were better than just dumping things when they happened. After they purchased their third home together, they crafted a set of responsibility guidelines called the "rEvolutionary Agreements" which are presented later.

CHILDREN

It was not known initially that Gail and Gregory were unable to have children. When Marian gave birth to Michael, it was as miraculous to the Hoags as to the bio-parents. They treated Michael as if he was also their son. While uncomfortable with this at first, Marian learned to see it from her son's perspective. She realized different types of love would make Michael a very well adjusted person. For example, he was much more physically playful with Gregory than anyone else. The Heads were also free to travel, go to movies or the mountains whenever they wished, as long as it fit the Hoags' schedule. Michael benefitted from four caring parents who offered unconditional love and consistent limits.

HOW THEY PAY THE BILLS

One account pays repair, mortgage and all related house bills. There is also a money drawer where everyone leaves receipts for food, and other shared consumables. Each couple is assigned a number of units to determine their fair monthly payment. Every adult counts for two units, so the Heads have five points since they have a child. The Hoags have four points. Any other persons temporarily staying in the house are also assigned two points each. Receipts and money owed are tallied by Marian, who handles household finances. Both couples also have their own joint accounts, plus various business accounts with one another and their other business partners.

HOW THEY EARN MONEY

A fascinating aspect of this multiple couple marriage is development of their many businesses. Initially, none of them worked together. At present, however, the Heads and Hoags have five thriving businesses, four of which are partnerships with each other. For instance, Gregory and Gail have a business producing self forming geometric puzzles. Marian and

Gail have a network marketing company. Gail, Marian and Glenn team as organizational consultants. Gail, Glenn and several others do executive team building. Glenn also has a worldwide snowboard company. If this wasn't enough, they are all pioneering a massive co-housing project in a small town outside of Boulder.

Chores

So who cooks for this menagerie? Each adult cooks one night a week. Whoever cooks, doesn't have to clean up. There are also friends who volunteer as guest chefs. Everyone still takes care of their own laundry and cleaning. One person shopping for five, rather than four shopping for five also makes life much easier.

Friends and Family

Initially, there was great concern from their parents. Over the years they've come to applaud the advantages of their childrens' lifestyle. The Hoags' parents have even become, what else,"co-grandparents"to Michael and see him as much as the Heads' parents.

When one couple has friends in town, the other can choose to widen its social circle. Parties are often spontaneous with a steady stream of business contacts and friends. What about criticism from outsiders? Reactions from other people have been favorable as far as they know. The exception was one couple who did not allow their child to return after a visit. The little boy came to the house to play with Michael. When the child's parents heard Michael had "two sets of parents" he was not allowed to return. When asked why, his mother admitted her discomfort with the dual couple marriage. Aside from this, however, they could think of no one who has shown distaste for their lifestyle. "On the contrary," Marian chimed in, "the more people find out about it, the more we are asked how they can do the same thing."

ADVANTAGES OF SHARED LIVING

Shared living offers far reaching benefits financially, socially, psychologically, spiritually and environmentally. Pooling resources and talents enables an intentional family to achieve much more than just one couple. By merging resources, several cars were eliminated until a third was recently purchased for emergencies. They have four separate computer terminals, but share just one printer, copier and fax. Operating five businesses at home under one roof means considerably less office expense and no drive time commute.

The Heads and Hoags have a strong commitment to the earth's ecology. They see shared housing as a future trend. Gregory cites religious groups in the U.S., such as the Amish, as an example of communal living styles that are more prevalent in other parts of the world. "What we have in this country, unfortunately, is mainly a separatist, lonely society where people don't usually know their neighbors, or work in trusting groups anymore. To survive, they compete for all available resources." Gregory hopes their unique "multicouple" marriage encourages others to explore the benefits for themselves.

The Heads' and Hoags' personal mission statement is, "to assist one another to fulfill our life's purposes plus contribute to the sustainability and evolution of all life on Earth." Obviously, living together in an intentional family marriage is not for everyone. Perhaps for a couple who cannot or does not want to have children, yet who don't wish to miss out on the experience, intentional family life may be a solution.

Many of us already live hundreds, even thousands of miles from our families of origin. Many of us consciously select people into our lives as substitute family. While we don't usually share the same residence with them, they frequently live nearby. Intentional family marriage links our extended family heritage of the early 20th Century with today's trend toward surrogate family membership. With economic and ecological forces as major global challenges ahead, more couples may want to explore the possibilities of co-housing and intentional family life.

7 Creating Your Own Love Style

Love styles enable couples to think outside the lines of conventional wisdom. A customized love style generates hope for relatively healthy couples who are being pulled under by their own white water currents. Typically, traditional therapy works on building communication skills. This alone, however, doesn't offer the rapid relief found in new redesigns when couples have already reached their limits. Couples on the brink of divorce frequently need a more radical way to reconstruct their lives. Once a new love style proves somewhat successful, couples are more likely to utilize traditional therapy, support and skill building.

So far we have discussed a variety of love styles which give couples the opportunity to salvage their marriages. These, however, are only helpful when both people are willing to explore alternatives. What happens when spouses don't choose to reconcile after field testing a particular redesign? What can be done to help them?

For example, Patricia and Joe already have had a successful Condo Couple Marriage for several years. Patricia spends weekends at Joe's condo. Recently, she has pushed to spend more time there, which was intrusive to Joe. He felt he shared his space enough with Pat, and her request really went too far. They remained in this power struggle, instead of in each other's arms, for an agonizing three months while the marriage began to slip away.

Finally, Patricia threatened divorce for extra leverage, but Joe saw through the bluff and called her hand. At this point, love style coaching suggested a new **TIME and TURF (TAT)** *design*. Joe and Patricia would still share weekends, (Friday at 6 p.m. till Sunday noon) but add a midweek evening on a short term basis. When time and turf battles are not resolved early, they can easily escalate into "Your Place, My Place or No Place." **Remember, balanced intimacy at each home base with sufficient time for independence is the desired goal.**

A *time limit strategy* is next employed for only one or two weeks. This way, a couple and their love style coach can assess how well a midweek time works for the short term. How does each person feel challenged? How is it different? Better? Worse? Is the new time frame working well enough to try for an entire month? Does the added midweek night satisfy Pat? Would any expanded midweek time work better for her, or do Wednesday nights need to be less frequent on alternate weeks for Joe to feel more comfortable? Any new **TAT** design requires this kind of fine tuning until Joe experiences sufficient autonomy, and Patricia enough intimacy. Other personal issues played out in the process, of course, also need to be tackled.

> *Just as a car's tires are balanced*
> *for a smoother ride, love style*
> *coaching rebalances a marriage's energetic flow.*

WHEN ALL ELSE FAILS

Of course, there may come a time when all reasonable efforts to rebalance intimacy and autonomy are exhausted. Here both spouses are offered the strategy of a *total relationship vacation* for at least one month followed by review. Then if each one chooses, they can begin another sequence with weekly calibrations until both are satisfied. **A total relationship vacation gives each person time to drop self righteous postures, and regain perspective of what, if anything, they really mean to one another.**

If all else fails, a **prolonged relationship vacation** of two or three months can also be negotiated. This usually does not include phone contact or in person meetings. Extended separation is followed by another overall review. Finally, if all reconciliation designs fail, one or both partners may elect to **discontinue**, so they can move on with their lives.

A cautionary note is appropriate here. Protracted separations of six months or longer generally result in parting company on a permanent basis. Research in this area serves notice that extended separation is not to be taken lightly. The basis for this finding appears to be twofold. First, biochemical levels of oxytocin (bonding hormone), dopamine, norepinephrine, and especially PEA (phenyl-ethyl amine), all drop off sharply. This love potion elixir no longer attracts or bonds the separated partners. Secondly, individuals surmount their fears of the unknown and begin to believe they can make it on their own. They start to trust that they will survive.

YOUR LOVE LIFE COMPASS

The love style best for you depends upon understanding your own and each others' LOVE LIFE COMPASS. This refers to one's balance points for **Intimacy with Autonomy and Commitment without Control.** As one partner moves psychologically closer, increased intimacy may start to feel more like dependency or subtle control to the other person. Loving energy which flows naturally when conditions are balanced, can quickly be diverted into self-serving control. It is suggested couples periodically check in to see if their

LOVE LIFE COMPASS is pointed in the direction they both fully intend to go. Mid course corrections are far better than going completely off course and hitting an iceberg. When this occurs, couples become emotionally frozen and like so many brave souls on the Titanic, go down with the ship. Without a LOVE LIFE COMPASS to chart the way, many couples are left rearranging deck chairs, while their Titanic relationship plummets to a watery grave.

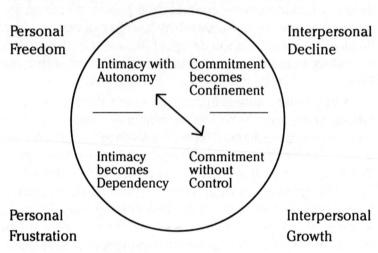

Personal Freedom

Interpersonal Decline

Intimacy with Autonomy

Commitment becomes Confinement

Intimacy becomes Dependency

Commitment without Control

Personal Frustration

Interpersonal Growth

How Much Togetherness?

How much time to spend together depends on you and your partner exploring what you both desire and fear about intimacy. You may need to experience these to an extreme to determine your own love life balance points. For example, Patricia and Joe needed to explore three extreme **TAT** designs. First, a week together at Joe's condo, then another full week at Patricia's apartment, followed by a vacation week with no contact. **This allows both to experience what they fear and desire most in order to clarify their needs.** If you and your lovemate are uncertain on how much time to spend together, the **EXTREMES** technique can break the logjam.

Joe will realize if he can survive seven days with Patricia, and explore his own counter dependency. Hopefully, Patricia will more accurately determine if her need for more closeness is sufficient, or feels too much and at what point. They will also better understand just what role each setting plays. **When a couple is given just three weeks to clarify their togetherness quotient, positive pressure, like a psychological tourniquet, helps stop the blaming.**

DIFFERENCES IN SEXUAL DESIRE

Sex therapy often deals with sexual frequency discrepancy. You only crave sex once a week, whereas your partner wants to make love at least five times a week. You feel imposed upon and emotionally withdraw from the demands, henceforth, the dance of intimacy and distancing begins. To clarify matters, a two week **EXTREMES** experiment is proposed. During the first week they agree not to have sex at all while the second week they agree to be sexual twice a day. **This way both experience what "too much" or "not enough" is like. Each person journals their reactions for discussion later. By experiencing "sexual extremes," you can usually discover the balance points of your sexual desire.**

Of course, many other approaches are very useful for couples to explore a happy sexual medium. They can pleasure themselves either with or without each other as an alternative to intercourse. Separate bedrooms is often another aphrodisiac for rejuvenated passion. Lovers may redecorate their rooms for special "fantasy evenings." One sexually playful wife turned her bedroom into a medical examination room where she got to play both nurse and doctor. Guess who had to be the "poor" patient? It was fun for them to also turn the tables for her reexamination later on. Different rooms, "taboo" semi public or natural outdoor settings are great fun and usher in new waves of energized passion. **Couples need to periodically consult their sexual**

compass to make sure each is "dialed in" for giving and receiving what they want.

TEN COMMANDMENTS
FOR CREATIVE TOGETHERNESS

What does a commitment to marriage really mean anymore? Traditional vows convey the fanciful belief, "for better or for worse, 'til death do us part." With marriages only lasting 6.4 years on the average, vows today convey more the notion of "for worse, 'til divorce do us part." Consequently, you and your loving partner may want to embrace a few new vows from the **Ten Commandments For Creative Togetherness** which, hopefully, enhance your chances to stay a loving couple.

TEN COMMANDMENTS
FOR CREATIVE TOGETHERNESS

1. The less my partner feels needed by me, the freer they are to love me.
2. The more my partner is sharing life with others, the more fascinating they become to me.
3. The more I express what I want to my partner, the less addicted I become to getting it.
4. The more open I am to unique forms for our relationship, the more my partner and I can be our unique selves.
5. The declaration "I love you" conveys that you empower me to unfold my fullest human potential.
6. The less my happiness depends on our relationship, the more joy we can share together.
7. The more responsibility I take in knowing who I am, the less I need my partner to look up my definition.
8. The more empowered I become, the less addicted I am to my partner and controlling their life activities.
9. The mutual give and take of power occurs when a sense of "we-ness" overrides the illusion of triumph over one's partner.

10. The more freedom my partner and I share in being ourselves, the more committed we feel to our relationship.

The **Ten Commandments for Creative Togetherness** support couples to enhance mutual intimacy and autonomy. They encourage love styles which nourish each person's potential. Therefore, "for better or for worse" might now mean you explore a duplex or weekend marriage before "divorce do us part." **Marital rigor mortis should never be declared until all options are considered and all hope has died.**

8 The Future of Marriage

THE ANNUAL RENEWABLE MARITAL AGREEMENT

Since the late 1980's, the United States Census Bureau reports divorce rates have leveled off at approximately 1.1 million per year. However, emotional and financial costs of even one divorce are still as devastating as ever, especially when it's your own. Courtroom guerrilla warfare in settlement and custody disputes is a high personal price for freedom. This remains true today even in no fault divorce states where courtrooms are still the sight of many gut wrenching contested divorces.

One dramatic way to end this dehumanizing marriage disposal system is by having an **Annual Renewable Marital Agreement (ARMA).** This is just like an annual physical checkup only this time one's marriage is the patient. The agreement becomes society's new legal sanction for marriage and divorce. ARMA requires the mutual consent and signatures of both spouses in order to continue a marriage for another year. When at least one spouse chooses not to renew during the 30 days prior to the anniversary date, the state discontinues the marriage. Divorce, with its tragic courtroom theater of the absurd would permanently be stricken from the docket by ARMA's more humane, affordable approach.

Discontinued marriages are subject to ARMA's universal marital agreement, which ensures co-responsibility of any future children, assets, or debts, and mediation if necessary. Physical custody and visitation are preset for five year intervals and then switched unless parents or mediation decide otherwise. ARMA also mandates two communication classes and three "clarification" counseling sessions before issuing anyone a marriage license. At least three "clarification" sessions are also required before the state **discontinues** any marriage. **No one files for divorce, is served papers or goes to court. No divorce stigma or legal expense is incurred.**

Starting January 1, 2002, or on a date thereafter, all marriages in America would be grandfathered into the ARMA system. Any divorce action still pending would be granted three added months to finalize before ARMA provisions took effect. A $50 fee would be split between county and state treasuries to record a couple's marriage or yearly renewal. **Fifty dollars is also the fee to discontinue.** If society requires an annual fee to renew automobile license plates, why not have one to renew a marriage license? ARMA's primary aim is to create a greater sense of immediacy and responsibility about one's choice to be a married person. Of course, if this seems too grand a scale, ARMA could be field tested in one or two states with only new marriages. Social assessment at one, two or three year markers might be conducted as well. Finally, if only piloted on a strictly voluntary basis, data would still be quite useful to any future considerations.

Benefits of ARMA

States would require a signed marital agreement, three "clarification" sessions and two classes before a marriage license is issued. This grants persons time to fully evaluate their decision as well as learn conflict resolution skills.

ARMA empowers spouses to make thoughtful decisions concerning renewal each year. All agonizing legal turmoil which frequently is more painful than the actual divorce is eliminated forever. Marital status inventories are mailed each year for spouses to fill out and discuss 90 days before their anniversary date. Inventories are brought to the annual marital check up. Two more "clarification" sessions are available if needed. Couples are reminded that not to decide is still a decision to discontinue. Any new love style options might be introduced here as well. Couples can also use other professional counseling resources at any time.

ARMA's mission is to promote marriage and family life getting better everyday, never taken for granted. While the pain of a broken home remains, courtroom drama, trauma and expense are gone forever. ARMA counseling becomes a part of health maintenance coverage under existing mental health insurance plans. Those who are uninsured are subsidized from the state's collection of annual ARMA fees. The projected $27 billion collected nationwide every year is diverted into conflict resolution classes, marriage enrichment and public education programs as well as marital research. It's like winning the Love Life Lotto. Only this time everyone and our country all win.

There surely will be those who claim an Annual Renewable Marital Agreement permits spouses to **discontinue** too easily. Unfortunately, divorce is already highly accessible. Most states have adopted no-fault statutes which typically take 90 days to finalize. Remember, divorce has already been the choice for nearly 50 million Americans over the past 100 years. With over a million more forecasted again this year and indefinitely into the future, we must consider practices which encourage more realistic, sustainable marriages. **In light of so many legal resources available to couples during divorce, a refocus on premarital assessment, conflict skills, clarification sessions, marriage enrichment and relationship redesigns is quite apparent.**

Consider the indelible imprint toxic marriages and divorces have already left on your children, parents, friends, practically every one of us. Consider the emotional baggage grown children from derailed families recycle through what will be the next generation of unsuspecting victims. **The new millennium is the ideal time to bravely rethink how people socially contract to spend the rest of their lives together as couples and families.**

An Annual Renewable Marital Agreement makes it clear you cannot just sleepwalk through your marriage vows. It encourages spouses to renew their lifetime commitment every year. **Even if ARMA legislation is never enacted, spouses and committed couples CAN STILL ACT AS IF IT WERE THE LAW: THEIR OWN.**

MARITAL AGREEMENTS

Much has been said about how trust is eroded by (pre)marital documents which delineate the distribution of joint marital assets and property in advance. Experience with such agreements has played to mixed reviews. Would-be spouses, women or men, totally terrified that divorce will bankrupt them, are given the assurance their rights and resources will be protected.

Often prospective brides feel that if their fiancé truly loved them, a (pre)marital loyalty test would not be needed. Previously divorced, disillusioned grooms, however, feel the necessity to protect their assets quite differently than first time idealistic brides, and vice versa. The preference for (pre)marital agreements by those once stung in divorce court is very understandable. However, prospective brides and grooms seem to feel less of an affront when the "pre" is dropped and just "marital" agreement is used. It appears "premarital" conveys a golddigger connotation, while "marital" doesn't. Therefore, a change to "marital agreement" might lessen some ill feeling about the practice. Courts would do well to consider this subtlety since it applies to conditions after the marriage. In 1999, the Colorado House of Representatives began debate on the benefits of premarital contracts for **all** future marriages. Under this contract all parties would "agree to undergo counseling, mediation or arbitration" before the state would recognize any marriage as "dissolved." This ripple effect of ARMA-like legislation will likely become a tidal wave before the New Millennium Love Style Revolution finally subsides.

COMMITTED COUPLE AGREEMENTS

Committed couples not electing marriage are strongly encouraged to still have some written agreement. This applies to sexclusive partners not presently choosing to marry, who may or may not live together. **It helps clarify how each committed couple wants to interpret Intimacy with Autonomy, Commitment without Control.** The agreement is also for couples who wish to explore relationship redesigns. While "shacking up" is not condoned, we must accept the overwhelming reality of 4.1 million live-in heterosexual couples. Their ranks increase by 100,000 every year. Hopefully, a Committed Couple Agreement offers helpful guideposts without moralizing about character or ethics. A significant portion will ultimately marry, once they begin to trust the field tested version. Regrettably, living together first does not reduce the staggering statistical toll of divorce. Nonetheless, it is hoped such an agreement alerts couples to what it takes to fulfill a sacred commitment.

While the sample agreement that follows looks legalistic, you may wish to draft a less formal one. Regardless, it is recommended that at least some descriptive statement of expectations be written, reviewed and amended as conditions change. There are committed couples who also faithfully renew their vows with a recommitment ceremony every year on their anniversary. While not married, they are traditional in every other respect, including strong spiritual and religious values. The main concern about unmarried couples is that they respect the rights and protections of any child they might bring into this world. Such a child deserves the complete legal safeguards of either marriage or adoption.

COMMITTED COUPLE AGREEMENT

This agreement is made this day month year by and between _____

(name) and (name),

who are referred to collectively herein as "partners."

The following agreement is entered into freely and states in terms of behavior, the Ten Commandment principles of Creative Coupling.

1. Partners agree to live together or in separate residences (whichever applies) throughout the relationship unless renegotiated.
2. Partners do not intend to procreate. In the event of pregnancy the female partner will choose, following consultation with her partner, an appropriate option of abortion, adoption or parenthood. Male partners will assume appropriate personal and financial responsibilities.
3. Partners have agreed not to marry, unless an infant is born, and a decision is made to raise the child in a traditional family.
4. Partners will fully disclose all pertinent sexual, health and birth control information prior to having a sexual relationship.
5. Partners agree to mutual STD and AIDS testing prior to sharing sexual intercourse. Birth control and safe sex practices will be used accordingly.
6. Partners agree to remain sexually monogamous unless their commitment ends.
7. Partners are liable for their own expenses and debts, unless otherwise negotiated or stated in respective wills, life insurance policies or health plans.
8. As a rule, partners will not combine finances unless they choose otherwise.

9.In the event one partner becomes disabled due to injury or illness, no financial liability is assumed by the other. Care of an incapacitated partner becomes solely a matter of personal choice. Healthcare insurance is the responsibility of each individual.

10.Loans between the partners are not advised but permitted with a signed, notarized statement.

11.Each person agrees to their partner's same and other sex friends. They will not act in a controlling manner in terms of these friendships, time apart, or otherwise.

12.Partners agree to review their balance of Intimacy with Autonomy every few months.

13.Both fully agree to reveal when any area of the relationship becomes toxic. Feedback is to be given at the earliest possible point before a concern threatens the integrity of the relationship. Partners will actively listen and mirror back for accuracy.

14.Each person agrees to never resort to physical violence, verbal abuse, or unwanted sex. Such an action will result in three couples counseling sessions and possible termination of the relationship.

In witness whereof, this Agreement is signed on the date first stated above in _____

(city)   (state)

Note: Feel free to customize your agreement to meet your own needs. This agreement is geared for either live-in or non-residential, unmarried, committed couples.

rEvolutionary Agreements
For Enlightened Living

The rEvolutionary Agreements developed by the Hoags and Heads for their intentional family marriage (Chapter 6), offer powerful guidelines for living a higher vision. They illuminate this path for us all.

rEvolutionary Agreements

1.Commit to the Mission:

Our mission is to liberate ourselves and all humanity to realize our full potential. I agree to use this mission as a guide to my actions.

2.Communicate with Integrity:

I agree to tell my truth, with compassion for myself and others.

3.Listen with your Heart:

I agree to listen respectfully to the communication of others and to receive their deepest meaning.

4.Honor One Another:

I agree to acknowledge that everyone, including myself, is making the best possible choice or decision we are capable of at that moment.

5.Appreciate Your Contributions:

I agree to take responsibility for acknowledging myself and receiving acknowledgment.

6.Express Appreciation for Others' Contributions:

I agree to acknowledge others.

7.Honor Our Differences:

I agree to come from a sense of cooperation and caring in my interactions with others, understanding that goals are often the same even though methods for achieving them may differ.

8. Use Grievances as Opportunities for Growth:

I agree to look for unresolved issues within me that create disproportionate reactions to others' behavior.

9. Maintain Harmony:

I agree to take the time to establish rapport, and then to re-connect with anyone with whom I feel out of harmony, as soon as it's appropriate.

10. Resolve Problems Constructively:

I agree to offer at least one solution any time I present a problem. I agree to take problems, complaints and upsets to the person(s) with whom I can resolve them, at the earliest opportunity. I agree not to criticize or complain to someone who cannot do something about my complaint, and I will redirect others to do the same.

11. Go For Excellence!

I agree to support others and to be supported in participating at the highest levels of excellence.

12. Learn From Experience:

I agree to look for opportunities to learn from my experiences, to continue doing what works and discontinue doing what does not work.

13. Be a rEvolutionary Leader:

I agree to foster an environment of genuine collaboration, in which all people, including myself, feel empowered to express our individual and collective potential.

14. Re-Evaluate Your Commitment:

I agree to choose and re-choose to participate in this rEvolution. It's my choice.

15. Lighten Up!

I agree to create joy in my relationships, my work and my life.

9   The New Millennium

Variety for men and women is imprinted in our genes. At all levels, cellular to societal, life seeks out new pathways to survive and expand. In marriage, familiarity often contributes to sameness. Everything begins to look and feel flattened out once married life loses its multi-dimensional texture. We wake up one day and sadly realize that our 20 year marriage has not really grown, but just recycled the same old year 20 times. Instead of viewing the crisis as an opportunity to deepen and grow together, we frequently choose to numb out and step out. We seek aliveness in the arms of someone new, but usually with the same old theme song playing in the background. If we just stood still long enough, what might we learn from love life's tumultuous transitions?

Marital autopsies have revealed a marital mid-life crisis phenomenon. Near the halfway point of marriages which end in divorce, something quite significant happens. At least one or both persons begin to withdraw from their commitment and often unknowingly prepare to exit. For a 20 year marriage ending in divorce, at least one partner can usually identify a personal shift roughly 9, 10 or 11 years into that marriage. Thus, the second half of the marriage is used in preparation for leaving the first half. This consistent finding across several thousand cases is viewed as the **Mid-Marriage Emotional Divorce or MED effect.**

Understanding **Mid-Marriage Emotional Divorce** in advance might alert couples to consider counseling and/ or a different love style, instead of insidious withdrawal from their mates. Also musical beds with other bodies in them is definitely not a solution to anything. Unfortunately, during such challenging times most couples limit their available options when they are needed most. They forget how important marital resuscitation is when a loving heart is dying from cardiac arrest. Regrettably, it's easier for them to remove all life support systems, and let the marriage slowly die, than to try a new prescription. This challenges us to honor our changing personal preferences while at the same time not diminishing our partner's. Creatively splitting up the time we share seems infinitely better than splitting up till the end of time, at least for married and committed couples who still care. As one ex-wife put it, "all I ever needed or wanted was a permanent, part-time, monogamous relationship. I only wish I had known this before my three marriages ended."

Those who choose not to leave when all vestiges of love have been removed, remain in what is best described as a **Zombie Marriage.** This marriage of the living dead is probably the closest experience to hell on earth. No matter how afraid you are of divorce, leaving is by far preferable to dying inside.

A Sneak Preview

So what will 21ˢᵗ Century marriages look like in terms of their social architecture? Are there patterns already emerging which will be the norm in the next millennium? *Love Styles* seeks to tap the public pulse as a pathfinder book and delineate some of the trends most likely in the next 40 or 50 years. For now, society is still unraveling from many unprecedented developments during the last half century of the previous millennium. For example, in 1950 no one prophesied "radical" marriages with separate beds, let alone separate bedrooms. In those times family and friends were initially shocked by such blatant disregard for matrimonial vows. To any casual observer, this meant the end of a couple's sex life, and inexorable demise of the marriage. Regrettably, this all too often became a self-fulfilling prophecy as pioneering love style couples started to doubt their own motives for being different. They had few if any sources of validation for what they honestly felt was best for them.

Precocious love style innovators went out on a limb without support of any safety net if they should falter. Even the innocent "reframing" of bed frames was sacrilege to some, seen as completely opposed to society's image of marital bliss. Gradually, however, such social architectural forays became more and more accepted. Today, mainstream marriages have also adopted his and her bathrooms, double sinks and medicine cabinets as well as his and her closets, hobby and TV rooms. Socially aware architects and builders are finally waking up to the fact that common sense solutions for shared space hassles also makes very good business sense.

Of course, the fun was only just beginning once the women's movement, feminism, birth control and sexual revolution all converged at the same 4-way intersection in the 60's. What a party it was from 1960 right through the 70's, when anyone could be sexual without fear of pregnancy or death. Once the genie was let out of the bottle, social experimentation and rebellion knew no bounds until the specter of AIDS shut down the festivities. Free love, drugs and rock and roll were celebrated for two decades as the era's own anthem. Open marriage and corporate marriages coexisted and at times even coalesced. Separate credit card marriages evolved once separate checking and saving accounts gained favor. It was not long before separate vacations came upon the scene, which some couples adopted along with their shared vacation times.

A brave new world of gender equality did indeed break all the rules, which in some instances was long overdue. What was once unthinkable, eventually found its way into a stunned and stoned society. The tragic war in Viet Nam further heightened the surreality of the times. When it all sorted out and the "smoke" lifted, marriage as an institution was still standing, although bruised, battered and forever altered.

Only a Nostradamus of Love could have crystal balled the El Niño effects on this country's love life landscape. Who could have imagined that by the year 2000, Americans would have grappled with: gender equality legislation, sexual harassment law, test tube pregnancy, sperm donor parenthood, single parent adoption, gay and lesbian parenthood and marriages, childless by choice marriages, the men's movement, relocated husbands for career wives, Viagra, breast and penile implants, coed military, prenuptial contracts, no-fault divorce and a Presidential impeachment sex scandal. Many events grew out of a sense of social injustice and rebellion along with startling advances in medical science. What was once outside mainstream society has been normalized today into America's psyche forever.

While the past 50 years fades into history's rearview mirror and the next half century rapidly approaches, what road map can safely guide us to Love Life Central in the year 2050? It is indeed likely that more flexible "couple friendly" strategies will evolve as the conventional marital mold continues to tarnish, rust and at times fall into disrepair. Rapid speed transport plus instantaneous mobile communication will allow relationships to stretch even further in time and distance. Combined with breakthroughs in biochemical nasal spray "love potions" and personal growth technologies, couples will be freer to breathe in everlasting love than ever before in human history.

At the dawn of space age lifestyles, we are quite likely to witness a decline in extramarital affairs, serial monogamy and even divorce as the benefits of Modular Marriage become more widespread. During the new century, Modular Marriage will offer a monogamous couple a lifetime supply of love style options, instead of a lifetime succession of committed mates. Social validation will grow for spouses who choose **Modular Monogamy** as they redesign intimacy with independence throughout their entire lives. Hopefully, this will also reduce the devastation of Mid-Marriage Emotional Divorces and extramarital affairs, as well as divorce itself.

What will modular rather than serial monogamy look like in real life terms, you may ask? One couple, for example, may start out living together in a traditional shared space marriage for seven years. They might then move apart into separate residences for five more years, followed by several years of seeing each other primarily on weekends and exotic vacations. Each may even eventually choose to purchase their own condominiums within easy walking distance of one another. Any children would, hopefully, be spared a toxic family life and the devastation of divorce. While the design of a couple's living style might change periodically, their mutual monogamy, trust, support and spiritual practice would never vary. Thus, modular married couples remain true both to their vows and their real estate agents for a lifetime of creative togetherness.

Freedom to redesign how time, space, distance and responsibilities are shared, can often re-energize our passion for one another. Even when couples remain in the same love style indefinitely, just knowing about other variations of optional togetherness can give a marriage that little extra edge it sometimes needs. The spark of perpetual courtship is kept alive. **Modular Monogamy** will gradually become an increasing part of our social fabric even though there will always be those threatened by change, even for the better.

Contrary to the movie "War of the Roses," most of us know disenchanted spouses who get along much better after they physically separate, even if it's within the same house. There are also those couples who later move back in together following their divorce and have a far better relationship, as do some creatively married couples who choose to live apart. Such atypical living styles sometimes occur even after adversarial divorce court "hired guns" have duked out the couple's personal destinies at high noon. If troubled spouses were given more permission to explore creative models of "spousal visitation," today's courtroom gunslingers might someday run out of ammo for their legalized ambushes.

Forecasting more flexible love styles and 21st Century Modular Marriages is in no way meant to trivialize our most sacred institution and societal building block. Modular Marriages are also not intended for spouses who have already been living in a virtual divorce for years, where children and adults are physically and emotionally at risk. We can only hope that such wounded families and couples safely discontinue.

For now, there seems to be one point we can all embrace. A horse and buggy will not carry us cross country on the interstate highway system any better than a 19th Century model of marriage will carry us through the 21st Century. Better models must continue to evolve. So sit back, buckle up, relax and enjoy the ride. If it's anything like the past 50 years, who knows what could happen? In fact, Modular Marriages and unique love styles which appear as radical today, will most likely be rather passé several decades from now with literally "20/20" hindsight. Traditional marital values, however, will remain just as strong and important as ever. Who knows? Husbands and wives may share separate residences on Mars and Venus, with romantic getaway rendezvous planned for the moon or even planet Earth.

A LOOK TO THE PAST

As long ago as ancient Rome, love's paradox of less time shared giving rise to lovers' passions, had its ancient beginnings. Sextus Propertius (54BC–2AD) was credited with the phrase, "Semper in absences felicior aestus amances" or simply, "absence makes the heart grow fonder."

In John Bartlett's 16th Edition of Familiar Quotations, we discover that Francis Davison's, "Poetical Rhapsody," from early 17th Century London, echoed the same sentiment. To be sure, more cynical views have also been expressed, such as "absence makes the heart grow fonder of somebody else," or "out of sight, out of mind." Ironically, such opposing sentiments can be equally true for any given couple at different seasons of their lives, as one's mind shifts in its orbital rotation around the heart.

However, throughout the ages the more romantic notion seems to have prevailed for couples who still care. James Howell's, "distance sometimes endears friendship, and absence sweeteneth it," Charles Hopkins reassurance to his sweetheart, "I find that absence still increases love," and Frenchman Laroche Foucault's, "absence diminishes little passions and increases great ones, just as the wind blows out a candle and fans the fire," are a few other 17th and 18th Century verses. More contemporary sentiments by Robert Lewis Stevenson, of *Treasure Island* fame, gleefully noted, "absences are a great influence in love and keep it bright and delicate." Quida, a 19th Century poet, once proclaimed, "the longest absence is less perilous to love than the terrible trials of incessant proximity." Finally, 20th Century journalist, Helen Roland, extolled this early feminist quandary, "failing to be there when a man wants her is a woman's greatest sin, except to be there when he doesn't want her."

As we enter the 21st Century, technology has radically transformed almost everything on the planet, but what about human nature? Are we so different today from our ancestors when it comes to romance, love and marriage? Or is love's enduring paradox, "absence makes the heart grow fonder" a profound, eternal truth which holds the secret for futuristic space age love styles? Hopefully, we'll find the answers soon, at least by the end of the new millennium.